ANTONIO LOBO

Marketing of Luxury Cruise Liners

ANTONIO LOBO

Marketing of Luxury Cruise Liners

Segmentation, Satisfaction and Future Patronage of Cruise Travellers

LAP LAMBERT Academic Publishing

Impressum/Imprint (nur für Deutschland/ only for Germany)
Bibliografische Information der Deutschen Nationalbibliothek: Die Deutsche Nationalbibliothek verzeichnet diese Publikation in der Deutschen Nationalbibliografie; detaillierte bibliografische Daten sind im Internet über http://dnb.d-nb.de abrufbar.
Alle in diesem Buch genannten Marken und Produktnamen unterliegen warenzeichen-, marken- oder patentrechtlichem Schutz bzw. sind Warenzeichen oder eingetragene Warenzeichen der jeweiligen Inhaber. Die Wiedergabe von Marken, Produktnamen, Gebrauchsnamen, Handelsnamen, Warenbezeichnungen u.s.w. in diesem Werk berechtigt auch ohne besondere Kennzeichnung nicht zu der Annahme, dass solche Namen im Sinne der Warenzeichen- und Markenschutzgesetzgebung als frei zu betrachten wären und daher von jedermann benutzt werden dürften.

Coverbild: www.ingimage.com

Verlag: LAP LAMBERT Academic Publishing AG & Co. KG
Dudweiler Landstr. 99, 66123 Saarbrücken, Deutschland
Telefon +49 681 3720-310, Telefax +49 681 3720-3109
Email: info@lap-publishing.com

Herstellung in Deutschland:
Schaltungsdienst Lange o.H.G., Berlin
Books on Demand GmbH, Norderstedt
Reha GmbH, Saarbrücken
Amazon Distribution GmbH, Leipzig
ISBN: 978-3-8383-6448-3

Imprint (only for USA, GB)
Bibliographic information published by the Deutsche Nationalbibliothek: The Deutsche Nationalbibliothek lists this publication in the Deutsche Nationalbibliografie; detailed bibliographic data are available in the Internet at http://dnb.d-nb.de.
Any brand names and product names mentioned in this book are subject to trademark, brand or patent protection and are trademarks or registered trademarks of their respective holders. The use of brand names, product names, common names, trade names, product descriptions etc. even without a particular marking in this works is in no way to be construed to mean that such names may be regarded as unrestricted in respect of trademark and brand protection legislation and could thus be used by anyone.

Cover image: www.ingimage.com

Publisher: LAP LAMBERT Academic Publishing AG & Co. KG
Dudweiler Landstr. 99, 66123 Saarbrücken, Germany
Phone +49 681 3720-310, Fax +49 681 3720-3109
Email: info@lap-publishing.com

Printed in the U.S.A.
Printed in the U.K. by (see last page)
ISBN: 978-3-8383-6448-3

TABLE OF CONTENTS

2

CHAPTER 1: STUDY ONE - SATISFACTION OF CRUISE TRAVELLERS

1.1   Importance of Service Quality

The new management buzzword Quality has taken the world by a storm. The last decade has witnessed the emergence of a wide variety of academic concepts on Quality, such as, Total Quality Management (TQM), Service Quality, Relationship Marketing and Total Quality Control (TQC). A characteristic feature of all these programmes is that they are customer focused and the satisfaction and loyalty created as a result offer a potential competitive advantage for the firm.

Organisations need to be aware of the various dimensions that their customers use to make judgements about service quality. According to Parasuraman, Zeithaml and Berry (1988) these dimensions are tangibles, reliability, responsiveness, empathy and assurance.

Superiority of the offer depends on customer's perception of service quality and not on the product's technical excellence or the service provider's perception of the offer. In recent years, despite good intentions, only a few service companies have been able to follow through on their commitment to satisfy customers. Service companies are beginning to understand that quality does not improve unless it is measured (Reichheld & Sasser, 1990).

Empirical research has identified a positive association between service quality improvements and market share (Buzzel & Wiersema, 1991). Increasing service quality has a potentially enormous impact on profitability, through reducing an organisation's operating cost and improving its market position. Service quality is increasingly being offered as the strategy for organisations to position themselves in the marketplace (S. W. Brown & Swartz, 1989; J.J Cronin & Taylor, 1992; Parasuraman, Zeithaml, & Berry, 1994)).

1.2 Star Cruises as the focal service organisation

The leisure cruise industry has been dominated for the past few decades by American and European cruise operators. Some of the large cruise companies are Carnival, Royal Caribbean, Celebrity, Crystal, Cunard, Holland America Line, Princess Cruises and Norwegian Cruise Line. In North America, 96% of the berths marketed are controlled by members of the New York based Cruise Line International Association (CLIA). In 1996, CLIA announced that it would spend US $ 30 million over a three year period on an unbranded, industry wide marketing

1

campaign. According to CLIA marketing director, Bob Sharack, this campaign was motivated by the cruise lines' ongoing push to compete with land-based vacations. Some 220 million people took vacations in 1995, but only 4.5 million cruised. (Murphy, 1996). CLIA members hoped to increase that figure to 8 million per year (by the Year 2000) by tapping that vast market : the 93% of North Americans who had never been on a cruise.

Potential clients are plagued with doubts and misconceptions about cruises. Many of them believe that cruises are an option only for newly-weds or senior citizens, and that they are generally meant for the rich. Unlike land-based resorts and tours, a cruise includes almost all of the costs involved in travelling. The ticket price covers meals, entertainment, sightseeing and often tips.

The leisure cruise industry is relatively new in the Asian region. However, it is growing rapidly and Singapore has taken the lead. The Singapore Cruise Centre recently upgraded at a cost of $ 23 million is now set on achieving a new target of becoming the number one cruise port in the world. Presently it has been rated number two after Port Everglades, Florida.("The Straits Times," 14 April 2000). In December 1998, Singapore welcomed its millionth passenger at the Singapore Cruise Centre after 7 years of intensive promotion. Singaporeans are increasingly seeing cruising as an attractive value-for-money vacation and lifestyle option. They go for short one-night or two-night getaways with family and friends. Industry figures show that the cruise business is expected to contribute at least $ 750 million a year to the tourism trade by the year 2004, a two-third increase in earnings over a period of nine years. ("The Straits Times," 14 April 2000)..

Star Cruises, which is the leading cruise line in Asia has a fleet of 9 cruise liners. In fact the combined gross tonnage of its 9 cruise liners makes Star Cruises one of the five largest cruise operators in the world today. Its latest megaship, the "Superstar Leo" which started operations in November 1998, has a capacity of 2800 passengers. Star Cruises are serviced by an international English speaking crew from over 25 nations. The safety, health and well-being of cruise passengers are its top priorities. It has one of the youngest and most modern fleet in the Asia Pacific region. Its customer philosophy and service culture is inherent in all its employees. Complaints are encouraged and travellers are invited to submit them in writing. Corrective and preventive action is taken in the earliest possible time.

The two strategies for enhancing customer's value and establishing a competitive advantage which have been identified in the marketing literature are cost advantage and differentiation (Day, 1990; Kotler, 1997; Porter, 1985). A firm can differentiate through quality, innovation and brand name. Lost cost advantage can be achieved through cheap labour, new technology and increased volume (Day, 1990). Marketing and financial experts constantly underline that hospitality operations should not only rely upon price competition. For example, Gamble and Jones (1991) argue that the hospitality industry in general should concentrate on improving their products and services in order to create a competitive advantage.

In order to determine service quality on cruise liners, cruise operators must be knowledgeable about the criteria and factors which their customers use and value when selecting a particular cruise. These factors are likely to include both product type characteristics like tangibles and physical attributes of the cruise liners as well as service type characteristics associated with liner personnel and on-board services. There is little published data about how travellers evaluate service quality on cruise liners. With the growing intensity of competition in this industry, it is vital that cruise operators clearly understand their customers' needs and act to meet them.

1.3   Objectives of the Study

The objectives of this exploratory study are fourfold, namely :

- to develop a customised instrument to measure the service quality onboard cruise liners.
- to compare and evaluate the effectiveness of SERVPERF vis-à-vis SERVQUAL as measures of service quality on board cruise liners.
- to compare and evaluate the effectiveness of the customised instrument vis-à-vis SERVPERF / SERVQUAL as measures of service quality on board cruise liners.
- To use the findings to improve the service quality on board cruise liners.

No previous empirical investigation available in the literature has attempted such a study of service quality on cruise liners.

1.4 Organisation of the Study

Chapter 1 (Introduction) addresses the importance of service quality, the context of the study, its objectives and an overview of what the study is expected to cover.

Chapter 2 (Literature Review) aims to provide a review of the literature on services marketing, service quality and satisfaction and links this to the service quality on board cruise liners.

Chapter 3 (Methodology) discusses the research design and statistical methods employed to develop and test the customised instrument.

Chapter 4 (Data Analysis) analyses the data, describes the findings and reports the results.

Finally Chapter 5 (Managerial Implications & Conclusion) discusses the managerial implications and limitations of the study.

CHAPTER 2: LITERATURE REVIEW

2.1 Services Marketing

Services are deeds, processes and performances. The core offerings of hospitals, hotels, cruises, banks and utilities comprise primarily deeds and actions performed for customers. Relying on the simple, broad definition of services, it becomes apparent that services are produced not only by service businesses such as those described above, but are also integral to the offerings of the producers of many manufactured goods. For example, car manufacturers offer warranties and repair services for their cars; computer manufacturers offer warranties, maintenance contracts and training; industrial equipment producers offer delivery, inventory management and maintenance services.

"That goods and services are different is generally agreed; what there is less agreement about is the way in which they differ and the extent to which these differences are relevant and significant from a marketing perspective" (Rushton & Carson, 1985). Three approaches which purport to distinguish between goods and services have been identified in the literature on services marketing (Goodfellow, 1983). The most widely cited differences which distinguish goods from services and which are common to most of the researchers are the intangibility of services, the heterogeneity of service outputs, the inseparability of producing and consuming services, and the perishable nature of services (Berry, Zeithaml, & Parasuraman, 1996; Rushton & Carson, 1985).

The second approach is the goods-services continuum classification proposed by Rathmell (1974) and Shostack (1978). Gronroos (1991) argues that while consumer packaged goods companies tend to focus on short term transaction, service companies cannot rely on single transaction but must seek relationships. The opposite ends on this continuum have been labelled as 'transaction marketing strategy' and 'relationship marketing strategy'. The degree of relationship marketing undertaken by the firm or desired by the customers is principally seen to be determined by the type of the products or business involved.

Figure 2.1 :   The transaction-relationship marketing continuum

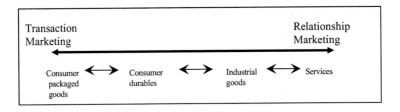

Source : Adapted from Gronroos C., (1991), The marketing strategy continuum – towards a Marketing concept for the 1990's, *Management Decisions,* Vol. 29, (December), No.1, Figure 1.

The proponents of the third approach believe that differences between goods and services disappear when the total market offer is considered ((J. R. Brown & Fern, 1981; Enis & Roering, 1981). They suggest that when viewing the differences between goods and services marketing, a more appropriate perspective may be the 'total market offering', which is the aggregate of all the benefits the customer receives as a result of the core offerings plus all the values added by members of the marketing channel.   It comprises both tangible and intangible aspects, regardless of whether the core offering is a good or a service.

One of the most basic concepts in marketing is the marketing mix, defined as the elements an organisation controls that can be used to satisfy or communicate with customers. The traditional marketing mix is composed of the four P's: product, price, place (distribution) and promotion (McCarthy & Perrault, 1993). These elements appear as core decision variables in any marketing text or marketing plan. The notion of a mix implies that all of the variables are interrelated and depend on each other to some extent. Further, the marketing mix philosophy implies that there is an optimal mix of the four factors for a given market segment at a given point in time. Services are usually produced and consumed simultaneously, and they are intangible. These facts have led service marketers to conclude that they can use additional variables to communicate with and satisfy their customers. For example, on a cruise ship, the design and décor of the liner as well as the appearance and attitudes of its employees will influence customer perceptions and experiences. Hence service marketers have adopted the concept of an expanded marketing mix for services, which includes, in addition to the traditional four P's, People, Physical Evidence and Process.

2.2 Customer Expectations of Service

Customer expectations are beliefs about service delivery that function as standards or reference points against which performance is judged. Thorough knowledge about customer expectations is critical to services marketers, because customers compare their perceptions of performance with these reference points when evaluating service quality. If a particular service company is wrongly informed about its customers' expectations, it could possibly lose its business to another company which hits the right target. This could also mean that the service company is spending money, time and other resources on things that do not matter to their customers. Some of the aspects of expectations that it needs to consider for successful marketing are as follows :

- What types of expectation standards do customers have about a particular company's services ?
- What are the most important factors which influence the formation of these expectations ?
- How can it meet or exceed its customers' expectations.

Service marketers need a thorough and clear definition of expectations in order to comprehend, measure and manage customer expectations (Zeithaml, Berry, & Parasuraman, 1993). Customer expectations can be measured by both qualitative and quantitative research. Qualitative methods such as customer focus groups, informal conversations with individual customers, critical incidents research and direct observation of service transactions, give managers the perspective that is critical in interpreting the data and initiating improvement efforts. Such research plays an important role in designing quantitative research, hence it is often the first type of research conducted. Basic research that relates to customers' requirements – that identifies the service features or attributes that matter to customers – can be considered expectation research. In this form, the content of customer expectations is captured, initially in some qualitative research. Quantitative research provides managers with data from which they can make broad inferences about customer expectations. This type of research quantitatively assesses the levels of customer expectations.

2.3 Customer Perceptions of Service

Customers perceive services in terms of the quality of service and how satisfied they are with their experiences. We assume that the dimensions of service and the ways in which customers evaluate service are similar whether the customer is internal or external (Gremler, Bitner, & Evans, 1994). External customers are those individuals and businesses that buy goods and services from the organisation. Internal customers are employees within the firm who, in their jobs, depend on others in the organisation for internally provided goods and services. When customer perception is referred to and how customers evaluate services, it is assumed that both internal and external customers are included and that the definitions, strategies and approaches can apply to either group.

Customer perceptions are measured both qualitatively and quantitatively. Qualitative research is exploratory and preliminary and are conducted to clarify problem definition and prepare for more empirical research (Bovee & Thill, 1992). Quantitative research in marketing, on the other hand, is designed to describe the nature, attitudes or behaviours of customers empirically and to test specific hypotheses.

2.4 Customer Satisfaction

Satisfaction is the consumer's fulfilment response. It is a judgement that a product or service feature, or the product or service itself, provides a pleasurable level of consumption-related fulfilment (Oliver, 1997). In other words, this definition means that satisfaction is the customers' evaluation of a product or service in terms of whether that product or service has met their needs and expectations. Failure to meet needs and expectations is assumed to result in dissatisfaction with the product or service. In conducting satisfaction studies, most firms will determine through some means (often focus groups) what the important features and attributes are for their service and then measure perceptions of those features as well as overall service satisfaction. Research has shown that customers of services will make trade-offs among different service features, depending on the type of service being evaluated and the criticality of the service (Ostrom & Iacobucci, 1995).

There are two conceptualisations of customer satisfaction in the literature : *transaction-specific* and *cumulative* (E. W. Anderson & Fornell, 1994). From the transaction-specific perspective, consumers make post-choice evaluation about their satisfaction with a specific purchase experience (Oliver, 1980). Cumulative customer satisfaction, in contrast, reflects the overall evaluation based on the total purchase and consumption experience with a service over time (E. W. Anderson & Fornell, 1994). The transaction-specific conceptualisation of customer satisfaction is meaningful for those who need diagnostic information about a

8

particular service encounter to monitor and improve service offerings. However, cumulative customer satisfaction is more relevant for managers interested in building long-term relationship with a stable customer base, because it provides a more fundamental indicator of consumers' global assessment and appreciation of the firm's past, current and future performance (E. W. Anderson & Fornell, 1994).

Quantitative research studies are essential for quantifying customer satisfaction, the importance of service attributes, the extent of service quality gaps and perceptions of value. Empirical data can highlight specific service deficiencies for deeper qualitative probing.

2.5 Service Quality

Service quality is a critical component of customer perceptions. In the case of pure services, service quality will be the dominant element in customers' evaluations. In cases where customer service or services are offered in combination with a physical product, service quality may also be very critical in determining customer satisfaction. Consumers judge the quality of services on their perceptions of the technical outcome provided and on how that outcome was delivered. For example, a restaurant customer will judge the service on his perceptions of the meal (technical outcome quality) and on how the meal was served and how the employees interacted with him (process quality)

The emerging empirical evidence suggests that quality affects business performance of industrial and consumer organisations in three major ways. Firstly, quality has an impact on manufacturing and operating costs in producing both goods and services. Hard evidence suggests that increasing quality can lead to significantly lower manufacturing costs (Fine, 1986; Garvin, 1988) and increased productivity (Deming, 1982). Second there is evidence to support relationship between price and perceived quality specially in cases where branding and product features are not significant (Gale, 1994). Quality allows a higher price to be charged but price also provides a quality indicator under some market conditions (Philips, Chang, & Buzzell, 1983). Thirdly, much of the empirical work using the PIMS data base has identified a strong positive association between quality improvements and market share gains (Morgan & Piercy, 1992).

Empirical evidence (Buzzel & Wiersema, 1991) also indicates that customer's perceptions of value are more effectively changed by raising quality than by lowering cost. Quality is therefore, increasingly being recognised as the key determinant of business success and the surest way to establish a competitive advantage (Bertrand, 1989; B. R. Lewis & Mitchell, 1990).

9

Conceptual Models for evaluating Service Quality

Lehtinen and Lehtinen's (1982) Quality Construct relates the three dimensions of quality viz. physical quality, interactive quality and corporate quality, with the elements of the service production process. Physical quality relates to the physical or tangible elements of the service such as physical products and physical supports. Interactive quality involves the interactive nature of the service and corporate quality is concerned with how the potential customers view the firm's image.

Gronroos (1984) service quality model comprises two main dimensions. The first of these is technical quality and it relates to what a customer receives as a result of his interaction with the firm. The second dimension is functional quality and it is concerned with how the service is delivered. This model is shown in Figure 2.2 below.

Figure 2.2 :   The service quality model by Gronroos (1984)

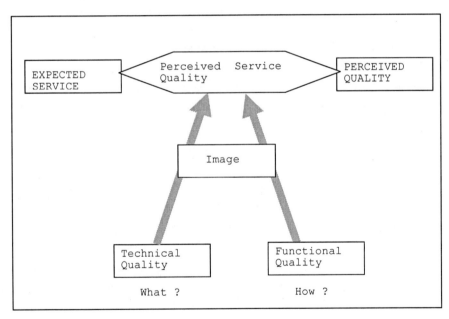

Parasuraman, Zeithaml and Berry's (1985) conceptual model of service quality (SERVQUAL) suggests criteria that consumers employ in evaluating service quality. This was based on a series of focus group interviews in service and retailing organisations using five service categories namely : appliance repair and maintenance, retail banking, long distance telephone, securities brokerage and credit cards. Ten determinants of service quality were originally identified and labelled as tangibles, reliability, responsiveness, competence, courtesy, credibility, security, access, communication and understanding. The authors subsequently (1988) recast the ten determinants of service quality into five specific components - tangibles, reliability, responsiveness, assurance and empathy.

Tangibles refer to the physical facilities, equipments, appearance of personnel and communication materials. Reliability is defined as the ability to perform the promised service dependably and accurately. Responsiveness is the willingness to help customers and to provide prompt service. Assurance is the knowledge and courtesy of employees and their ability to convey trust and confidence. Empathy refers to the caring individualised attention the firm provides to customers. These five dimensions of service quality captured the facets of all the ten originally conceptualised dimensions. Based on empirical evidence, Parasuraman et al (1988) claim that these dimensions of service quality are applicable across a wide spectrum of industries. They have defined service quality as the extent of discrepancy between customers' expectations and their perceptions of the firm's performance based on the five dimensions. Their conceptual model of service quality typically views the service quality construct as being closely related to, yet distinct from the issue of satisfaction.

Expectations and perceptions, which play a significant role in the conceptual model are linked through Oliver's (1981) disconfirmation of expectations paradigm. This paradigm holds that the predictions customers make in advance of consumption act as a standard against which customers measure the firm's performance later. This model defines the process that generates the expectations and perceptions in terms of the service quality dimensions and the methodology for measuring service quality. Zeithaml et al (1993) state that customers have many sources of information that lead to expectations about the upcoming service encounters with a particular company. Their perceptions of the firm's performance, on the contrary, are the result of the four internal gaps within the organisation identified by Parasuraman et al (1988) in their gaps model shown on the next page.

11

Figure 2.3 :   The service quality model by Parasuramam, Zeithaml and Berry

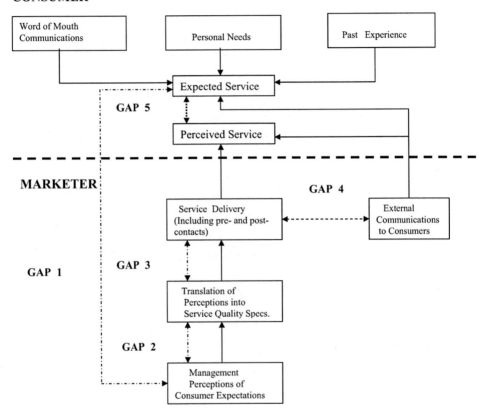

Source : Parasuraman A., Zeithaml V.A., and Berry L.L., (1985), A conceptual model of
service quality and its implications for future research, *Journal of Marketing*, Vol.49, (April),
p44, Figure 1.

Building on the dimensions of service quality, Parasuraman et al (1988) have also developed an
instrument called SERVQUAL, for quantitatively measuring perceived service quality. This
instrument measures customers' expectations and perceptions relative to the five determinants of
service quality and it reveals the quality gap.

The SERVQUAL instrument consists of three sections. The first one measures customers' expectations of the service. It comprises a set of 22 items covering the five dimensions of reliability, responsiveness, tangibility, assurance and empathy. The second section comprises the same 22 items for measuring the service provider's perceptions of service quality. The respondents are required to indicate on a seven point likert scale the extent to which they agree or disagree to the stated questions. The third section is aimed at obtaining the relative weightages for the five quality dimensions in a particular service context.

Performance Measure - SERVPERF

The multi-dimensional model of Parasuraman et al (1985; Parasuraman et al., 1988) SERVQUAL, has been widely accepted as the most comprehensive model for establishing the service quality construct (Boulding, Kalra, Staelin, & Zeithaml, 1993; Carman, 1990; J.J Cronin & Taylor, 1992). Both Lehtinen and Lehtinen's (1982) and Gronroos (1984) models mentioned earlier do not propose any systematic method of measuring service quality nor do they prescribe reasons for quality gaps within the organisation.

SERVQUAL has nevertheless come under severe criticism from various service marketing researchers. Carman (1990) and Babakus and Boller (1992) argue that the five dimensions cannot be generalised across a wide spectrum of industries. They suggest adding a few more dimensions from Parasuraman, Zeithaml and Berry's list of five, depending on the type of industry. Vandamme and Leunis (1992) caution against using SERVQUAL to service categories which have little elements in common with services already investigated with this instrument.

A study was done to examine the discriminant validity of SERVQUAL (Teas, 1993). In it three important limitations of the scale were raised. Firstly, considerable variance in the respondents' interpretations of SERVQUAL's "should" or expectations measure implied that a considerable amount of the variance in service quality expectations was a result of different interpretations of the questions being asked, and not the result of different respondent attitudes and perceptions. Secondly, a relatively large number of respondents interpreted the expectations question to involve a question about the attribute importance. For them, the use of the Perceptions - Expectations framework was inappropriate as in this situation, holding performance constant, perceived quality would increase with decreasing levels of attribute importance. Thirdly, a number of respondents interpreted the expectation measures to involve questions about 'forecast' or predicted performance levels. In this respect, the (P-E) perceived quality framework lacked discriminant validity with respect to the disconfirmed expectations component of consumer satisfaction models. The author further states that given the confusion associated with respondents' interpretation of the expectations measure and the lack of discriminant validity between the expectations measure and the other expectation concepts used in marketing, it might be useful to consider modifying the perceived service quality framework.

McDougall and Levesque (2000) used the SERVQUAL instrument to measure the service quality of retail banks. Factor analysis was performed separately on the SERVQUAL results based on the P-E scores and on SERVPERF, the unweighted perception component of SERVQUAL. It was found that results obtained using SERVPERF were superior to those obtained using SERVQUAL. This gives evidence that expectation scores do not contribute significantly towards measuring service quality. Cronin & Taylor (1992) concluded through their empirical investigation that SERVPERF outperformed the unweighted SERVQUAL in predicting behavioural intentions. SERVPERF seemed to display better discriminant and nomological validity properties. Similarly Bolton and Drew (1991) have argued that customer perceptions of continuous services (e.g. telephone services) may depend solely on performance.

2.6 Satisfaction versus Service Quality

The terms satisfaction and quality seem to be used interchangeably by both practitioners and writers. However, researchers have attempted to be more precise about the meaning and measurement of the two concepts, resulting in considerable debate. There is growing consensus that the two concepts are fundamentally different in terms of their underlying causes and outcomes (Parasuraman et al., 1994). Although they have certain things in common, satisfaction is generally viewed as a broader concept while service quality focuses specifically on dimensions of service. Based on this view, perceived service quality is a component of customer satisfaction. Service quality reflects the customer's perception of specific dimensions of service, such as reliability, responsiveness, assurance, empathy and tangibles. Satisfaction, on the other hand, is more inclusive: it is influenced by perceptions of service quality, product quality, price as well as situational and personal factors.

2.7 Service Quality in the Cruise Industry

The quality of services produced on a cruise liner is a critical factor in providing a differential advantage for a cruise line over its competitors. However, to determine service quality, cruise lines must primarily identify the criteria and factors which their customers use to evaluate the quality of their cruise.

There is hardly any published data associated with the measurement of service quality on cruise liners. However, studies on service quality have been undertaken in similar hospitality operations such as airlines, hotels and tourism industries.

McKenna (1990) studied more than 4000 frequent flyers and concluded that route structure is the most important criteria in choosing an airline, followed by price and reliability.

Gourdin and Kloppenborg (1993) used SERVQUAL to conclude that customers and management do not give the same importance ratings to the different criteria when selecting airlines. They thus confirmed that a service quality gap (Gap1) exists between customer expectations and management perceptions of those expectations in the airline industry. Carlson (1987) performed an extensive study in the Scandinavian Airlines (SAS). This airline placed the responsibility for ideas, decisions and actions with those employees who came in contact with customers. These employees included ticket agents, flight attendants, baggage handlers and all other frontline employees. These contacts, or "moments of truth" ultimately determined whether SAS would succeed or fail. In a customer-oriented company the traditional hierarchical corporate structure had begun to change. The organisation became decentralised with responsibility being delegated to those who were previously at the bottom of the corporate organisational pyramid. This system allowed problems to be solved on the spot. When SAS first instituted this new system, the middle managers became hostile and counterproductive because they were confused about their new role. Eventually, however, their role was clarified. Middle managers actually were essential in the smooth functioning of a decentralised organisation.

Lewis (1994) conducted surveys covering 66 attributes in six U.S. hotels. He identified the basic constructs that affect hotel guests' lodging choice and guests' perceptions of hotels. He concluded that attribute importance varied according to the type of hotel and the travel purpose. He also measured the gaps between U.S. hotel management and consumer expectations and perceptions. Eight gaps were identified and analysed.

Atkinson (1988) conducted a survey to determine the importance of 59 attributes used by guests to select a hotel and to assess how well individual properties measured up to guests' expectations. Mehta and Vera (1990) surveyed 194 guests in a Singapore hotel, comparing their perceptions of 26 attributes and contrasting these perceptions across a number of market segments. They concluded that the key attributes used in selecting a hotel differed in each market segment.

Barsky and Labagh (1992) proposed a customer-satisfaction matrix as a tool for evaluating guest information and attitudes and for identifying related strengths and weaknesses. Yu (1992) presented a case study of a hotel rating system as a service quality mechanism. Reid and Sandler (1992) examined the use of technology to improve service quality in the hotel industry.

Chadee and Mattson (1996) attempted to measure the quality of tourist experiences and how different quality factors affect the global satisfaction of tourists.

Fick and Ritchie (1991) proposed the SERVQUAL model as an instrument for the measurement of service quality in four major sectors of the travel and tourism industry, i.e. airlines, hotels, restaurants and ski area services.

Le Blanc (1992) identified six factors related to customer perception of service quality in travel agencies. These factors are corporate image, competitiveness, courtesy, responsiveness, accessibility and competence.

A cruise liner can be likened to a floating hotel. A person wishing to travel on a cruise needs to make a booking with the cruise line or a travel agent. He/she has to be present at the cruise centre on the day of departure of the cruise and go through immigration and other formalities. Once on board the cruise liner the traveller would need various types of services. These are related, among other things, to the accommodation, food & beverage, entertainment, shopping, safety and places of destination. At the end of the cruise, which could last for a few days, the traveller has to disembark from the liner. In order to determine the overall service quality of a particular cruise line, a traveller would need to evaluate the various service attributes related to the entire cruise. In this study seventy five attributes of service quality on board cruise liners have been identified.

The literature review has revealed that although there is a well established body of work associated with service quality in hospitality operations like those in airlines, hotels and tourism industries, there is no published data available regarding service quality on cruise liners. This research study would therefore endeavour to close this obvious gap in the literature.

CHAPTER 3: RESEARCH METHODOLOGY

3.1 Development of Questionnaire

The three instruments used in this study are the 22-item SERVQUAL, SERVPERF and a customised instrument.

The 22-item SERVQUAL scale developed by Parasuraman et al (1988) was used in its entirety. However, amendments in the wording and phrasing of some of the items were made to reflect the special nature of services produced by Star Cruises. Each of the 22 items had to be rated on a 7 point Likert scale for both the expectation and perception scores. The SERVPERF instrument used in this study simply consisted of all the perception statements included in the 22-item SERVQUAL.

Relevant literature and focus group techniques were used to develop the customised instrument. 2 focus groups interviews were held with people who had travelled on Star Cruises and one focus group interview was held with the marketing personnel of Star Cruises. Each of these focus groups consisted of five to six persons. The groups were asked to discuss the attributes of services on cruise liners which they considered important and essential. Schiffman and Kanuk (1997) recommend usage of the focus group technique in the early stages of attitude research.

A 75-item customised instrument was developed as an outcome of the focus group interviews. 22 of these items closely matched with those already included in the SERVQUAL.

It was decided to obtain expectation and perception ratings on a 7 point Likert scale for all of the 75 items of the customised instrument.

3.2 Design of the Questionnaire

The final questionnaire as shown in *Appendix 1* consisted of the 75-item customised scale. Against each of these items, respondents were required to rate (on a 7 point Likert scale) their expectations of a high performing cruise line and also their perceptions of services provided by Star Cruises. SERVQUAL and SERVPERF ratings were obtained from the first 22 items of the customised instrument. This was deliberately done so as to avoid making the questionnaire too lengthy.

3.3 Pilot Study

Seven persons who had previously travelled on cruise liners were involved in the pilot test which was conducted to detect and clarify any mistakes and ambiguity in the questionnaire. A small number of typing errors and ambiguous statements were rectified. Also, initially the expectation and perception statements were typed out on separate pages. This made the questionnaire rather lengthy and tedious for the respondent to complete. It was thus decided to group both the expectation and perception statements thus considerably reducing the length of the final questionnaire.

3.4 Sampling Plan

It was decided to use a non-probability sampling method (convenience sampling) owing to time and cost factors. Also a sample size of approximately 300 seemed adequate as this number was consistent with previous studies undertaken on service quality in the hospitality area. It was assumed that travellers who had recently experienced a cruise would be better able to provide meaningful responses as compared to those who had taken a cruise a long while ago. In the interest of smooth and adequate collection of data it was necessary for the interviewers to be trained. This was done one week prior to the actual cruise date. Well-trained interviewers must be familiar with all the words in all the questions and must understand all the instructions in the questionnaire. In addition, they must be familiar with the general purpose of the study, who is sponsoring it, how the sample was selected and how the data would be coded, analysed and published. The training was conducted in three stages, i.e. briefing by the study director, reading the questionnaire and practice interviews. The practice interviews generally uncovers various types of anticipated responses, and a major task of the interviewer training consists of learning what to do when each of these responses is encountered. Several discussion sessions were held, during which problems were reviewed, question by question, with the study director and all the interviewers. At these discussions, interviewers were free to ask general questions, such as how to probe or what to do with a respondent. The four trained interviewers (with the permission of Star Cruises) joined a 4 day cruise on the megaship "Superstar Leo".

3.5 Collection of Data

The "Superstar Leo" sailed out of Singapore Port on a 4 day cruise with approximately 2000 passengers on board. The trained interviewers distributed survey questionnaires to the passengers on the second day of the cruise. A detailed explanation was given to each of the respondents regarding the purpose of the survey and also where the completed questionnaire had to be deposited. As a small incentive to complete the questionnaire every respondent was given a keychain as a souvenir from Star Cruises. A total of 300 questionnaires were distributed. Although this number seems small in relation to the total number of passengers on the cruise, it must be noted that majority of them were travelling either with their families (57.4%) or in a group (41.6%).

A box was placed at the reception counter for respondents to drop the completed questionnaires prior to their departure. Before the cruise ended at Singapore on the 4th day, an announcement was made on the public address system gently reminding passengers about the survey questionnaires.

3.6 Statistical Tools Used

Factor analysis is a statistical technique which is used to condense many variables into a few underlying constructs (Hedderson & Fisher, 1993). It reduces a large number of attributes by combining them into meaningful groups or factors.

Before factor analysis can be used as a data reduction method, it must satisfy the underlying assumption of sampling adequacy (Norusis, 1993). The Kaiser-Meyer-Olkin (KMO) was used as a measure of sample adequacy for this study.

Next the principal component (PC) method of factor extraction was used. This method is appropriate when the analyst is primarily concerned about prediction or the minimum number of factors needed to account for the maximum portion of the variance represented in the original set of variables. It is also useful when the factor analyst has prior knowledge suggesting that specific error and variance represent a relatively small proportion of the total variance (Hair, Anderson, Tatham, & Black, 1995).

Varimax Rotation method was employed to rotate and identify the factor loadings of each variable. This method is one of the three major orthogonal approaches which have been developed, the other two being Quartimax and Equimax. If the goal of the research is to reduce the number of original variables, regardless of how meaningful the resulting factors may be, the appropriate solution would be an orthogonal one. Also, if the researcher wants to reduce a larger number of variables to a smaller set of uncorrelated variables for subsequent use in a regression or other prediction technique, an orthogonal solution is the best (Hair et al., 1995).

19

The original 5 SERVQUAL dimensions (factors) was used for comparative purposes throughout the analysis.

As the customised instrument had a large number of variables, the roots criterion method was not suitable to extract the number of factors. Hence, an alternative method, Cattel's scree plot was used instead. The scree plot method involves graphically plotting eigenvalues against the number of factors. The optimum number of factors to be extracted is determined by the elbow on the curve joining all the eigenvalues.

Factor loadings are analogous to the co-relation (or a set of co-relations) of the original variables with the factor. Thus each factor loading is a measure of the importance of the variable in measuring that factor. Gorsuch (1983) advocated that factor loadings of 0.3 are sufficient as a criterion of meaningfulness.

To detect for the existence of any possible correlation, Pearson's correlation coefficient was used to measure the strength and direction of linear association between the explanatory variables.

Multiple regression was used to test the effectiveness and reliability of each of the three instruments used to measure the service quality of Star Cruises. The dependent variable used was the overall service quality rating of Star Cruises, while the explanatory variables were the dimensions of factors associated with each of the three instruments. The corresponding Coefficient of Determination, R^2 , found from the regressions were used to compare the explanatory power of each instrument. R^2 refers to the proportion (per cent) of the total variation in the dependent variable (overall service quality) that is explained by the set of explanatory variables (service quality dimensions). Effectively, R^2 measures the goodness of fit of a model.

To counter the problems of artificially high R^2 caused by few observations in the sample or more independent variables included in the multiple regression equation given a fixed number of observations (overfitting), the adjusted R^2 incorporates the effect of including independent variables in a multiple regression equation. It is an important summary statistic to evaluate how well the multiple regression model fits the data (Watson, Billingsley, Croft, & Huntsberger, 1993).

Reliability analysis was done to measure the reliability of the three scales. Values of Cronbach's Alpha above 0.7 are usually regarded as sufficient evidence that the scale has acceptable reliability.

CHAPTER 4: DATA ANALYSIS AND FINDINGS

4.1 Sample Profile

Out of the 300 questionnaires distributed, 202 were returned. However, 12 of these had to be discarded due to incompleteness. The overall response rate (67.3%) was considered satisfactory as the questionnaire was quite lengthy.

Table 4.1 : RESPONSE RATE

Questionnaires	Frequency	Percent
Given Out	300	100%
Returned	202	67.3%
Discarded	12	4.0%

4.2 SERVQUAL

4.1.1 Mean Expectation and Perception

Table 4.2 on the next page summarises both the expectation and perception scores pertaining to the 22-item SERVQUAL scale. The means of the 'Expectation' scores are arranged in descending order and the corresponding 'Perception' scores are shown with their rank order in the extreme right column. As seen from the table, the mean expectation score ranges from 5.15 to 6.70, with '1' being 'strongly disagree' and '7' being 'strongly agree'. Respondents had high expectations on all the 22 items of the SERVQUAL scale.

Table 4.2 : EXPECTATION & PERCEPTION MEANS FOR 22 ITEMS

Item No.	Item	Expectation "A High Performing Cruise Line will ....."		Perception " Star Cruises....."		
		Mean	Std Dev	Mean	Std Dev	Rank
17	Have employees who are competent in performing their duties.	6.71	0.62	5.73	1.06	8
16	Have courteous and polite employees	6.66	0.65	6.08	1.12	3
15	Make passengers feel safe	6.64	0.61	5.97	0.94	4
2	Have attractive ambience and décor on their ships	6.61	0.59	6.31	0.80	1
12	Have employees who are always willing to help	6.58	0.65	5.77	0.84	7
22	Meet the needs of special passengers,e.g. elderly, handicapped, etc.	6.58	0.71	4.96	1.12	20
3	Have employees with professional appearance	6.56	0.63	5.78	1.05	5
11	Have employees who provide prompt services	6.53	0.62	5.67	0.92	10
10	Have employees who are concerned, responsive and attentive to passengers' needs	6.51	0.58	5.69	0.95	9
14	Have employees who instill confidence	6.49	0.70	5.54	0.98	12
6	Handle complaints from passengers promptly	6.44	0.65	5.49	0.98	14
1	Have a modern fleet of ships	6.43	0.76	6.28	0.87	2
21	Have employees who are sympathetic and reassuring when passengers encounter problems	6.38	0.66	5.33	1.00	16
5	Have employees who meet passengers' requests in a reasonable time	6.35	0.67	5.59	0.90	11
13	Have employees who always find time to meet passengers' requests	6.34	0.67	5.49	0.87	13
19	Have convenient arrival/departure times	6.24	0.99	5.78	1.05	6
8	Meet needs of passengers correctly upon first request	6.14	0.79	5.33	0.95	15
9	Carry out passengers' requests or instructions without error	6.03	0.81	5.33	0.89	17
18	Have employees who pay individualised attention to passengers	5.92	0.97	5.05	1.02	19
20	Have employees who understand the needs of different nationalities	5.90	1.17	5.15	1.05	18
7	Have employees who rarely make mistakes	5.63	1.03	4.93	1.02	21
4	Charge low fares for the cruises	5.15	1.36	4.63	1.20	22

On the other hand, the mean perception score for the 22 items ranges from 4.63 to 6.31. All the items except items 20,21 and 22 were rated 5 and above. This may suggest that there are

22

opportunities in various aspects of the services offered by Star Cruises.

Table 4.3 : DIFFERENCE SCORES FOR 22 ITEMS

	Mean	Std Deviation
Have a modern fleet of ships	-0.14	0.90
Have attractive ambience and decor on their ships	-0.30	0.83
Have convenient arrival/departure times	-0.46	1.20
Charge low fares for the cruises	0.51	1.65
Have courteous and polite employees	-0.57	1.07
Make passengers feel safe	-0.66	1.02
Have employees who rarely make mistakes	-0.69	1.02
Carry out passengers' requests or instructions without error	-0.70	0.91
Have employees who understand the needs of different nationalities	-0.74	1.34
Have employees who meet passengers' requests in a reasonable time	-0.76	0.99
Have employees with professional appearance	-0.78	0.95
Meet needs of passengers correctly upon first request	-0.80	1.00
Have employees who are always willing to help	-0.80	0.81
Have employees who are concerned, responsive and attentive to passengers' needs	-0.82	0.96
Have employees who always find time to meet passengers' requests	-0.85	0.90
Have employees who provide prompt services	-0.86	0.82
Have employees who pay individualised attention to passengers	-0.86	1.03
Handle complaints from passengers promptly	-0.94	1.07
Have employees who instill confidence	-0.95	1.04
Have employees who are competent in performing their duties	-0.97	0.97
Have employees who are sympathetic and reassuring when passengers encounter problems	-1.04	1.08
Meet the needs of special passengers encounter problems (e.g. elderly, handicapped, infants, etc)	-1.61	1.20

The Perception-minus-Expectation scores shown in the above table further justifies the need for Star Cruises to improve its operations. The difference scores of all the 22 items were negative, indicating the existence of a service quality gap. This implied that the performance of Star Cruises on these SERVQUAL items were below the expectation of the respondents. The mean difference scores had a range between −1.61 and −0.14.

4.1.2 Dimensions Scores

Table 4.4 : FACTOR SCORES FOR EXPECTATION

Dimension	Mean	Std Deviation
Assurance	6.62	0.52
Responsiveness	6.48	0.55
Tangibles	6.22	0.53
Empathy	6.20	0.63
Reliability	6.15	0.58

Table 4.5 : FACTOR SCORES FOR PERCEPTION

Dimension	Mean	Std Deviation
Assurance	5.83	0.78
Tangibles	5.72	0.61
Responsiveness	5.64	0.76
Reliability	5.35	0.78
Empathy	5.25	0.74

Table 4.6 : DIFFERENCE SCORES FOR THE FIVE DIMENSIONS

Dimension	Mean	Std Deviation
Tangibles	-0.50	0.68
Assurance	-0.79	0.74
Reliability	-0.79	0.75
Responsiveness	-0.83	0.69
Empathy	-0.94	0.76

The scores of the original 5 dimensions of SERVQUAL (Tangibles, Reliability, Responsiveness, Assurance and Empathy) were computed by summing up the mean score of each item within each dimension and dividing the total mean score obtained by the number of items in that particular dimension.

The peception scores for Assurance and Tangibles received the highest ratings. The unweighted difference scores between expectation and perception (gap) were all negative. The highest difference was for Responsiveness and Empathy, which indicates that Star Cruises have to pay more attention to these 2 dimensions.

4.1.3 Reliability Analysis

Table 4.7 : RELIABILITY ANALYSIS OF SERVQUAL

Cronbach Alpha (α)	
Assurance	0.81
Responsiveness	0.81
Reliability	0.79
Empathy	0.72
Tangible	0.60

The Expectation scores were used for the purpose of Reliability Analysis. All the 5 dimensions of SERVQUAL seemed to have relatively good internal consistency as measured by the Cronbach Alpha. Tangibles had the lowest score.

4.1.4 Correlations

Table 4.8 : COR. COEFFICIENT (r) OF SERVQUAL WITH OVERALL SQ

SERVQUAL Dimensions	Overall Service Quality (r)
Tangibles	0.54
Reliability	0.65
Responsiveness	0.58
Assurance	0.48
Empathy	0.43

r > 0.234 for significance at 1% level

All the five dimensions of SERVQUAL were significantly correlated with Overall Service Quality.

4.1.5 Multiple Regression

Table 4.9 : MULTIPLE REGRESSION – SERVQUAL

SERVQUAL Dimensions	B	Beta	t	Sig T
Tangibles	0.05	0.03	2.06	0.03*
Reliability	0.29	0.28	13.34	0.02*
Responsiveness	0.23	0.21	10.84	0.08
Assurance	0.21	0.28	8.64	0.38
Empathy	-0.02	-0.02	-0.16	0.91

F =61.67	Sig. F = .000
* significant at 5% level	

When the 5 dimensions were regressed on the overall evaluation, the adjusted R^2 obtained was 0.181. The resultant output from the multiple regression yielded two significant dimensions at the 5% significance level – Tangibles and Reliability. However, there is the problem of correlated independent variables, which means that when all other variables are accounted for, the contribution of say Tangibles or Reliability beyond this is not significant, i.e. the contribution of Tangibles or Reliability is captured through the other independent variables which they are related to. Further research is necessary to understand the complicated causal relationship between the dependent and independent variables.

4.3 SERVPERF

4.3.1 Perception Means and Dimension Scores

The SERVPERF scale consists of the perception items of SERVQUAL including its 5 dimensions. These have been recorded in Table 4.2 previously, hence it will not be discussed here.

4.3.2 Reliability Analysis

Table 4.10 : RELIABILITY ANALYSIS OF SERVPERF

	Cronbach Alpha (α)
Assurance	0.87
Responsiveness	0.83
Reliability	0.75
Empathy	0.72
Tangible	0.64

The perceptions scores for the 22 items were used for the purpose of Reliability Analysis. As the Cronbach Alphas for the 5 dimensions are above 0.6 the analysis is acceptable. Previous studies using SERVQUAL (Carman, 1990; Finn & Lamb, 1991) have yielded Alphas ranging from 0.59 to 0.93.

4.3.3 Multiple Regression

Table 4.11 : MULTIPLE REGRESSION – SERVPERF

SERVQUAL Dimensions	B	Beta	T	Sig T
Tangibles	0.26	0.19	2.21	0.02*
Reliability	0.16	0.15	1.52	0.12
Responsiveness	0.22	0.20	1.95	0.05
Assurance	0.06	0.05	0.60	0.54
Empathy	0.09	0.08	0.86	0.38

F = 21.515   Sig. F = .000

* significant at 5% level

The adjusted R^2 obtained as a result of regressing the 5 dimensions of SERVPERF with the overall service quality of Star Cruises was 0.370. This is significantly higher than the value of R^2 obtained using SERVQUAL. Only one dimension, Tangibles, was found to be significant (at 5% level) in explaining the variance in the overall evaluation of service quality of Star Cruises.

4.4 CUSTOMISED SCALE

4.4.1 Mean Expectation and Perception

75 items pertaining to the service quality of Star Cruises were generated, out of which 22 items were from the SERVQUAL scale. The 'perception-minus-expectation' score in descending order is shown in the table below :

Table 4.12 : DIFFERENCE SCORES FOR ITEMS OF THE CUSTOMISED SCALE

Items of the Customised Instrument	Percep. Mean	Std Dev	Expect. Mean	Std Dev	P – E Mean	Std Dev
Have good Casino and Jackpot facilities	5.40	1.10	4.79	1.79	0.61	1.79
Be punctual in departure and arrival time	6.59	5.23	6.42	0.79	0.17	5.19
Have good photo gallery facilities	5.37	1.21	5.37	1.29	0.00	1.38
Have clean and well maintained ships	6.51	0.69	6.57	0.69	-0.06	0.73
Have good sports and fitness facilities	6.16	5.25	6.28	0.85	-0.12	5.38
Have a modern fleet of ships	6.28	0.87	6.42	0.76	-0.14	0.90
Have ships which behave well whilst sailing, thus reducing chances of sea-sickness	6.37	0.94	6.54	0.71	-0.17	1.08

27

Have wide passage ways for easy movement	5.84	0.91	6.07	0.84	-0.23	1.11
Visit many ports of destinations	5.32	1.09	5.57	1.12	-0.26	1.25
Have attractive ambience and decor on their ships	6.31	0.80	6.61	0.58	-0.30	0.83
Show care and concern for passengers when the cruise do not depart or arrive on time	5.87	4.56	6.17	0.78	-0.30	4.52
Have good cabin maintenance and cleaning facilities	6.23	0.85	6.56	0.70	-0.33	0.95
Have ships which are comfortable to sail on	6.29	1.02	6.63	0.66	-0.34	1.04
Have good video arcade facilities	5.29	1.21	5.63	1.35	-0.34	1.54
Have employees who are energetic looking	5.86	1.11	6.21	0.89	-0.35	1.05
Have prompt meal and beverage services	5.91	0.99	6.34	0.83	-0.43	0.97
Have convenient arrival/departure times	5.78	1.05	6.24	0.99	-0.46	1.20
Have some staff on board ship who can speak other major languages besides English	5.44	1.05	5.91	0.01	-0.47	1.11
Provide accurate voyage information on board ships	5.77	0.93	6.27	0.75	-0.50	1.02
Have good safety records and ISM certification	6.22	0.91	6.73	0.64	-0.51	0.78
Charge low fares for the cruises	4.63	1.20	5.14	1.36	-0.51	1.65
Have reliable baggage handling facilities	5.69	1.00	6.20	0.89	-0.51	0.97
Receive strong support from its travel agents	5.59	1.29	6.15	0.87	-0.56	1.41
Have courteous and polite employees	6.08	1.12	6.65	0.65	-0.57	1.07
Have hassle-free pre-boarding security screenings	5.60	0.98	6.21	0.78	-0.61	0.94
Make passengers feel safe	5.97	0.94	6.63	0.60	-0.66	1.02
Provide amenities (e.g. extra pillows, blankets, towels, etc) to passengers	5.77	0.99	6.43	0.77	-0.66	0.86
Have good passenger accounting and billing facilities on board ships	5.67	0.92	6.35	0.73	-0.68	0.85
Have employees who rarely make mistakes	4.94	1.02	5.63	1.03	-0.69	1.02
Carry out passengers' requests or instructions without Error	5.33	0.89	6.03	0.81	-0.70	0.91
Serve adequate snacks in between meals	5.22	1.11	5.94	1.00	-0.72	1.17
Handle reservation services efficiently	5.58	1.05	6.32	0.66	-0.74	1.07
Have employees who understand the needs of different nationalities	5.15	1.05	5.89	1.17	-0.74	1.34
Have employees who meet passengers' requests in a reasonable time	5.59	0.90	6.35	0.67	-0.76	0.99
Have good signs, posters and instructions for easy movement on their ships	5.62	1.14	6.39	0.68	-0.77	1.18
Have employees with professional appearance	5.78	0.98	6.56	0.63	-0.78	0.95
Meet needs of passengers correctly upon first request	5.33	0.95	6.13	0.78	-0.80	1.00
Have employees who are always willing to help	5.77	0.84	6.57	0.65	-0.80	0.81
Have employees who are concerned, responsive and attentive to passengers' needs	5.69	0.95	6.51	0.58	-0.82	0.96
Have spacious rooms to sleep and relax comfortably	5.54	1.16	6.37	0.87	-0.83	1.40
Have good security arrangements	5.85	0.84	6.69	0.55	-0.84	0.79
Have employees who always find time to meet passengers' requests	5.49	0.87	6.34	0.67	-0.85	0.90
Have employees who provide prompt services	5.67	0.92	6.53	0.62	-0.86	0.82
Have employees who pay individualised attention to passengers	5.05	1.02	5.91	0.97	-0.86	1.03
Have proper lost baggage procedures	5.39	0.88	6.25	0.77	-0.86	1.04
Inform travellers of any delays to the cruise departures well in advance	5.71	0.91	6.58	3.61	-0.87	3.66
Provide courteous telephone service	5.31	1.28	6.23	0.77	-0.92	1.25
Handle complaints from passengers promptly	5.49	0.98	6.43	0.65	-0.94	1.07

Have fast and efficient check-in and check-out facilities	5.48	1.23	6.42	0.72	-0.94	1.16
Treat passengers fairly without any bias	5.74	1.04	6.69	3.61	-0.95	3.71
Have employees who instill confidence	5.54	0.98	6.49	0.70	-0.95	1.04
Have employees who are dependable in their service delivery	5.55	1.01	6.52	0.74	-0.97	1.02
Have employees who are competent in performing their duties	5.73	1.06	6.70	0.62	-0.97	0.97
Have good medical and health services	5.55	0.89	6.52	0.71	-0.97	1.01
Conduct proper Safety Drills to demonstrate procedures in cases of emergencies	5.58	1.06	6.58	0.75	-1.00	1.06
Have good child care facilities on board	5.16	3.15	6.20	1.18	-1.04	3.29
Have employees who are sympathetic and reassuring when passengers encounter problems	5.33	1.00	6.37	0.66	-1.04	1.08
Have good communication (telephone, fax, internet) facilities	4.93	2.68	5.98	1.07	-1.05	2.77
Be flexible and bend rules for its passengers	4.48	1.27	5.60	1.08	-1.12	1.32
Have convenient ticket reservation system	5.61	1.03	6.75	1.16	-1.14	5.20
Have good arrangements for shore excursions	5.14	1.20	6.37	0.80	-1.23	1.24
Provide a variety of beverages on the cruise	4.93	1.36	6.18	0.94	-1.25	1.34
Impose few restrictions when travellers' cruise plans are changed (e.g. deposit will not be forfeited, no fines imposed etc.)	4.44	1.24	5.83	1.08	-1.39	1.48
Have good shows and entertainment for adults	5.12	1.11	6.51	0.83	-1.39	1.26
Provide a variety of main courses of food that passengers can choose from	4.84	1.14	6.28	0.77	-1.44	1.22
Have a good selection of magazines, newsstudys and books on board	4.51	1.41	6.01	0.97	-1.50	1.46
Have good entertainment facilities for children	4.80	1.41	6.38	2.25	-1.58	2.57
Have good gift and duty free shops	4.40	1.29	5.99	1.00	-1.59	1.37
Meet the needs of special passengers encounter problems(e.g. elderly, handicapped, infants, etc)	4.96	1.12	6.57	0.71	-1.61	1.20
Serve food that is fresh	5.10	1.20	6.76	0.57	-1.66	1.24
Have good arrangements for viewing the ship's bridge and other places of interest on the ship	4.60	1.53	6.40	0.79	-1.80	1.64
Provide food that caters to needs of different passengers (e.g. vegetarian food, halal food, baby food, low fat/ calories, diabetic diet etc)	4.69	1.28	6.53	0.85	-1.84	1.47
Serve delicious and tasty food	4.71	1.24	6.59	0.68	-1.88	1.41
Make timely and clear announcements	4.48	1.54	6.58	0.68	-2.10	1.59
Offer frequent traveller programmes	3.62	1.78	5.88	1.00	-2.26	1.60

The difference scores of all except the first 3 items were negative, indicating the existence of a service quality gap. The mean difference scores had a range of between –2.26 and 0.61. This implies that the performance of Star Cruises on the 72 items were below the expectations of the respondents. This is usually the case with these types of studies, particularly owing to the high expectations that travellers have of a brand new cruise liner.

4.4.2   Factor Analysis

The Kaiser-Meyer-Olkin (KMO) value obtained for the customised instrument was 0.8913. This figure is considered to be extremely good for a factor analysis model (Kaiser, 1974). Due to the large number of items, Cattel's scree test was used to determine the number of factors to be extracted. The scree plot seems to suggest a 4-factor solution since there is a sudden reduction in the gradient of the slope after the fourth point on the horizontal axis. After subjecting the data to a Varimax Rotation, 40 items were retained from the original 75 items. This is shown in table 4.13 below. The 4 factors explained 50.62% of the total variance as shown in table 4.14.

Table 4.13 : FACTORS DERIVED FROM THE CUSTOMISED SCALE

Factor	Items	Factor Ldg	EXPECTATION		PERCEPTION	
			Mean	Std.Dev	Mean	Std.Dev
Factor 1	Meet needs of passengers correctly upon first request	0.80	6.14	0.79	5.34	0.96
	Have employees who provide prompt services	0.74	6.53	0.62	5.67	0.93
	Carry out passengers' requests or instructions without error	0.74	6.03	0.81	5.33	0.90
	Have employees who are competent in performing their duties	0.73	6.71	0.62	5.73	1.07
	Handle complaints from passengers promptly	0.72	6.44	0.65	5.49	0.99
	Have courteous and polite employees	0.68	6.66	0.65	6.08	1.13
	Have employees with professional appearance	0.66	6.57	0.64	5.78	0.99
	Have employees who are sympathetic and reassuring when passengers encounter problems	0.63	6.39	0.66	5.34	1.01
	Have employees who always find time to meet passengers' requests	0.62	6.35	0.67	5.50	0.88
	Have employees who pay individualised attention to passengers	0.60	5.92	0.97	5.05	1.02
	Have employees who are always willing to help	0.59	6.58	0.65	5.78	0.84
	Have employees who rarely make mistakes	0.59	5.63	1.03	4.94	1.03
	Have employees who meet passengers' requests in a reasonable time	0.56	6.35	0.67	5.59	0.91
Factor 2	Provide food that caters to needs of different passengers (e.g. vegetarian food, halal food, baby food, low fat/ calories, diabetic diet etc)	0.71	6.54	0.85	4.69	1.29
	Serve food that is fresh	0.71	6.76	0.58	5.10	1.21
	Provide a variety of beverages on the cruise	0.68	6.19	0.94	4.93	1.37
	Provide a variety of main courses of food that passengers can choose from	0.66	6.29	0.78	4.85	1.15
	Have good arrangements for viewing the ship's bridge and other places of interest on the ship	0.64	6.41	0.80	4.60	1.54
	Serve delicious and tasty food	0.61	6.60	0.68	4.71	1.24
	Have good shows and entertainment for adults	0.57	6.52	0.84	5.12	1.12
	Have good Casino and Jackpot facilities	0.55	4.78	1.79	5.41	1.11
	Serve adequate snacks in between meals	0.53	5.95	1.00	5.22	1.12
	Have good arrangements for shore excursions	0.50	6.38	0.81	5.14	1.20
Factor 3	Have clean and well maintained ships	0.78	6.58	0.69	6.52	0.69
	Have ships which are comfortable to sail on	0.66	6.64	0.67	6.30	1.02
	Have a modern fleet of ships	0.65	6.43	0.77	6.29	0.88
	Have good cabin maintenance and cleaning facilities	0.56	6.57	0.71	6.24	0.86
	Have attractive ambience and decor on their ships	0.56	6.61	0.59	6.31	0.80
	Have ships which behave well whilst sailing, thus reducing chances of sea-sickness	0.56	6.54	0.71	6.36	0.94
	Have spacious rooms to sleep and relax comfortably	0.48	6.38	0.87	5.55	1.17
	Have good photo gallery facilities	0.41	5.37	1.29	5.38	1.21
	Have fast and efficient check-in and check-out facilities	0.39	6.43	0.72	5.48	1.23
Factor 4	Have convenient ticket reservation system	0.79	6.76	1.17	5.61	1.03

30

Receive strong support from its travel agents	0.68	6.15	0.87	5.59	1.29
Have hassle-free pre-boarding security screenings	0.67	6.23	0.79	5.61	0.99
Handle reservation services efficiently	0.60	6.34	0.67	5.59	1.05
Inform travellers of any delays to the cruise departures well in advance	0.51	6.59	3.62	5.72	0.91
Have proper lost baggage procedures	0.50	6.26	0.78	5.39	0.88
Offer frequent traveller programmes	0.46	5.89	1.00	3.63	1.79
Are punctual in departure and arrival time	0.25	6.42	0.80	6.60	5.23

Table 4.14 : VARIANCE EXPLAINED BY THE FACTORS

Factor		Eigenvalue	Percentage of Variance explained	Cumulative Percentage of Variance explained
Factor 1	Liner Service Personnel	12.81	32.04%	32.04%
Factor 2	On-board Services	3.18	7.97%	40.01%
Factor 3	Operational Features	2.48	6.21%	46.23%
Factor 4	Supplementary Services	1.75	4.39%	50.62%

The first factor was relatively simple to interpret as all the 13 items in this factor related to the employees of Star Cruises. This was therefore named "Liner Service Personnel"

The second factor had 10 items which were associated with the food and beverage, entertainment and gambling facilities on board. Hence it was named "On-board Services"

9 items in the third factor belonged to the "Operational features" of Star Cruises.

Lastly the 4th factor had 8 items which were associated with "Supplementary Services" such as ticket reservation system and baggage handling.

Table 4.15 : FACTORS SCORES OF THE CUSTOMISED SCALE

Factor		Customised Instrument	
		Mean	Standard Deviation
Factor 3	Operational Features	6.04	0.61
Factor 1	Liner Service Personnel	5.50	0.71
Factor 4	Supplementary Services	5.46	1.03
Factor 2	On-board Services	4.97	0.83

The above mean scores were derived from the perception ratings. The highest mean rating of 6.04 was given to 'Operational Features' whereas 'On-board Services' was rated the lowest at

4.97. This indicates that Star Cruises have significant opportunities for improvement, especially with regards to their onboard services such as dining and entertainment.

4.4.3   Reliability Analysis

Table 4.16 : RELIABILITY ANALYSIS OF THE CUSTOMISED SCALE

Cronbach Alpha (α)	
Liner Service Personnel	0.92
On-board Services	0.86
Operational Features	0.79
Supplementary Services	0.52

The perception ratings were used for the purpose of Reliability Analysis of the Customised Scale. The above Cronbach Alpha values of the 4 factors confirms that the customised scale is of acceptable reliability.

4.4.4   Correlations

Table 4.17 : COR. COEFFICIENT (r) OF CUSTOMISED SCALE WITH OVERALL SQ

Factors of Customised Scale	Overall Service Quality (r)
Liner Service Personnel	0.68
On-board Services	0.41
Operational Features	0.40
Supplementary Services	0.16

r > 0.196 for significance at 5% level

All the factors of the Customised Scale except Supplementary Services were significantly correlated with Overall Service Quality.

4.4.5   Multiple Regression

The 4 factors were regressed on the overall evaluation of service quality using the perception scores as shown in Table 4.18 on the next page. This gave a R^2 value of 0.429. Two factors – 'Liner Service Personnel and 'Operational Features' were significant at 1% level. However, there is the problem of correlated independent variables, which means that when all other variables are accounted for, the contribution of say Liner Service Personnel or Operational Features beyond this is not significant, i.e. the contribution of Liner Service Personnel or Operational Features is captured through the other independent variables which they are related

32

to. Further research is necessary to understand the complicated causal relationship between the dependent and independent variables.

Table 4.18 : MULTIPLE REGRESSION – CUSTOMISED SCALE

Factors	B	Beta	T	Sig T
Liner Service Personnel	0.39	0.33	4.18	0.00*
On-board Services	0.10	0.09	1.40	0.16
Operational Features	0.47	0.34	4.70	0.00*
Supplementary Services	-0.04	-0.05	- 0.86	0.38

F = 34.31   Sig. F = .000

* significant at 1% level

4.5 Comparison of the 3 Instruments used in the Study

Table 4.19 : COMPARISON OF CRONBACH ALPHA OF THE 3 SCALES

SERVQUAL		SERVPERF		CUSTOMISED SCALE	
Dimensions	Cronbach Alpha (α)	Dimensions	Cronbach Alpha (α)	Factors	Cronbach Alpha (α)
Assurance	0.818	Assurance	0.874	Liner Service Personnel	0.929
Responsiveness	0.812	Responsiveness	0.830		
Reliability	0.795	Reliability	0. 758	On-board Services	0.864
Empathy	0.722	Empathy	0.722	Operational Features	0.799
Tangible	0.606	Tangible	0.641	Supplementary Services	0.528

Table 4.20 : COMPARISON OF REGRESSION ANALYSIS OF THE 3 SCALES

	SERVQUAL	SERVPERF	CUSTOMISED SCALE

Adjusted R^2	0.181	0.370	0.429

Table 4.19 on the previous page is useful for the purposes of comparison of the Cronbach Alpha values of the 3 scales. Similarities were observed in the values obtained by using SERVQUAL and SERVPERF. The dimension of Assurance had the highest coefficient whereas that of Tangibles had the lowest in both the scales.

The factors of the customised instrument (except for Supplementary Services) had higher reliabilities than the dimensions of both SERVQUAL and SERVPERF.

Table 4.20 on the previous page ranks the 3 scales using the adjusted R^2 values in the following order : Customised instrument, SERVPERF and then SERVQUAL. Additionally, the 4 factors of the customised instrument explained 50.62% of the variance.

It is clear that in the measurement of service quality onboard cruise liners, SERVPERF performed better than SERVQUAL. This is consistent with studies undertaken previously by Bolton and Drew (1991) and Cronin and Taylor (1992).

Also, the 4 factors of the customised instrument with a total of 40 items could be usefully employed to measure service quality of cruise liners.

CHAPTER 5: CONCLUSION, IMPLICATIONS & RECOMMENDATIONS

5.1 Conclusion

The hospitality industry has long been aware of customer satisfaction (CS) and service quality (SQ) as critical determinants of market competition and retention. Although companies in this industry have conducted several research studies on CS and SQ, they have only recently introduced systematic instruments like SERVQUAL and SERVPERF to measure CS and SQ. Researchers have not evaluated these instruments rigorously especially in the study of service quality associated with the hospitality industry. Academic researchers and industry practitioners have obtained mixed results when using these instruments. This study was therefore conducted to contribute to the advancement of CS and SQ in the hospitality industry, in particular the luxury cruise industry. It provided compelling empirical evidence that among the three instruments considered, the customised instrument is the most appropriate basis for measuring CS and SQ in the luxury cruise industry. More specifically the major findings of this study can be summarised as:

SERVPERF outperformed SERVQUAL in the areas of reliability and model fit. Hence there is doubt on the usefulness of SERVQUAL in predicting overall satisfaction on cruise liners. These findings were similar to those of Cronin and Taylor (J.J Cronin & Taylor, 1992; 1994) who concluded through their empirical investigation that SERVPERF outperformed the unweighted SERVQUAL in predicting behavioural intentions. In their study SERVPERF seemed to display better discriminant and nomological validity properties. It was also evident from the findings of this study that the customised instrument which was especially developed for the liner cruise industry was more effective in measuring SQ than both SERVQUAL and SERVPERF.

Factor analysis of the attributes in the customised instrument yielded 4 factors, the dominant one being 'Liner Service Personnel' which explained a major portion of the variance (32%). This factor (dimension) comprised of 13 attributes which were all associated with service personnel of the cruise liner. Individually, this factor could be more useful than each of the five dimensions of SERVQUAL and SERVPERF, owing to the fact that in a purely service-oriented industry like cruises, people and processes are extremely important elements of the services marketing mix.

This finding was in line with the findings of Carman (1990) and Babakus and Boller (1992) who argue that the five dimensions of SERVQUAL cannot be generalised across a wide spectrum of industries.

The following dimensions of the three instruments used were significant in explaining the variances in the overall SQ of Star Cruises :

SERVQUAL   - Tangibles and Reliability

SERVPERF   - Tangibles

Customised Instrument- Liner Service Personnel and Operational Features (this dimension is associated with the tangible component of the service offering).

The above findings reveal that there is a heavy emphasis on 'Tangibles' for SERVQUAL and SERVPERF which contradicts the emphasis on 'Service Personnel' for the customised instrument. The reason for this is that SERVQUAL has very limited questions relating to Service Personnel. When respondents are not asked adequate questions about a particular dimension of the service offering, they tend to give less importance to that dimension. In other words, if there are no pointed questions about certain attributes, respondents generally tend to ignore them. The customised instrument on the other hand, included a wide variety of questions relating to Service Personnel. Here the respondents were conscious of the related attributes, hence they gave appropriate feedback. This finding has been apparent in several other studies (including those in the retailing business) where service front line and operational staff play a very important role in the overall service quality.

The perception-minus-expectation (service quality gap) scores were least on tangible items like clean and well maintained ships, modern fleet and good sports and fitness facilities. This was owing to the fact that the cruise liner on which the survey for this study was undertaken was a very modern megaship, and one of its only kind operating out of Singapore port. At the bottom end, where the service quality gap was most prominent, were items like delicious and tasty food, timely and clear announcements and frequent traveller programme. Star Cruises need to take appropriate action to reduce the gaps on these items. Food is always a delicate issue in the leisure industry and more so on a cruise liner.

Majority of the respondents gave very high ratings to their expectations of the service offering.

This was possibly due to the survey being conducted on a brand new cruise liner, hence the expectations of the respondents were naturally very high. This being the case, the 'expectation' data had very limited value when analysing responses of cruise travellers.

This study has achieved several objectives which were established at the outset. First, the primary purpose of this study was to develop a customised instrument to measure service quality on board luxury cruise liners. Second, this study assessed the three CS and SQ instruments for their relative validity and reliability. This purpose was successfully achieved by identifying the customised instrument as the most desirable instrument for CS and SQ research in the luxury cruise industry.

5.2 Implications

The results of this study have several important implications.

It provided a desirable direction in relation to the use of the customised instrument for future CS and SQ studies in the hospitality and cruise industries. It has elaborated on the conceptualisation and operationalisation of the determinants of customer satisfaction – the customers being cruise travellers. By adopting the customised instrument researchers and managers may be able to obviate confusions from using multiple scales. The customised instrument can also prove valuable to cruise operators for measuring CS more reliably, hence preventing them from relying on other less reliable paradigms for developing strategies.

Cruise operators can obtain more accurate, complete and useful diagnostic information that can facilitate the improvement of service quality on board cruise liners. By measuring the perception-minus-expectation gaps on the various attributes, the underlying service problems can be detected and appropriate recovery measures can be taken. Cruise operators who are committed to improving customer satisfaction can gain more confidence from this study such that their investment will be rewarded with satisfied customers.

The customised instrument offers an excellent opportunity for a performance-based assessment of CS and SQ, as Cronin and Taylor (1992; J.J. Cronin & Taylor, 1994) argued, because it requires cruise companies to measure performance perceptions along with other variables. A well managed internal marketing system can be established so that cruise operators can consistently enjoy high customer perceptions on all the attributes of service quality.

Finally, it is hoped that this study will reinvigorate more intensive research studies in this important area, especially in the luxury cruise and hospitality industries. Although these measurements were focused on attributes associated with cruise liners, they can be adjusted to accommodate a broad range of other related service sectors, such as hotels, airlines and the tourism industry.

5.3 Limitations and Suggestions for Future Research

Although the overall results of this study are quite encouraging, their interpretations may be limited by several considerations.

The results cannot be generalised across the entire cruise and hospitality industries. This study collected data from travellers on a modern cruise liner. Hence the sample may not represent the entirety of cruise travellers. There could be substantial differences in the perceptions of travellers sailing on older cruise liners. Similar studies should be replicated by including more diversified subjects which may then increase the chances of generalising the results. The sample drawn for this study was not purely random. The sample basis should be broadened by including more cruises in different parts of the world. Future studies should design more systematic sampling in order that the sample can better represent the population.

Simultaneous measurement of expectations and perceptions could possibly bias the results of this study. Although research supports the reliability of this simultaneous measurement method (Johnson, Anderson, & Fornell, 1995), measuring expectations at different times could have produced more reliable results.

Generally, researchers recommend that expectations should be measured prior to the initiation of an actual consumption experience, although there is no firm evidence in the literature for resolving the question of when expectations should be measured. In this respect it is possible that the Expectancy Disconfirmation (EDM) approach may be more appropriate. EDM relies on customers' direct, subjective comparisons called subjective disconfirmation, which is believed to mediate expectations and perceptions towards CS. This is measured by asking respondents to directly compare perceptions to expectations using a "better-than or worse-than" scale (Oliver,

1981; Swan & Trawick, 1981). The expectations in this study were operationalised as a normative comparison standard following the work of Parasuraman et al (1988). Woodruff, Cadotte and Jenkins (1983) suggested that there are many forms of expectations. Measurement of different kinds of expectations may produce varying results. Determination of any particular type of expectation to be measured for the luxury cruise industry should be an important topic for future research.

With 75 attributes incorporated in the study, the length of the questionnaire might have made it a tiring task for some respondents to complete. This may have resulted in some respondents misrepresenting their actual expectations and perceptions of the various attributes of service quality. The findings of this survey could have been supplemented by the findings of in-depth interviews conducted on board the liner with travellers who were randomly selected.

Future research needs to pay more attention to the effects of prior experience and travel purposes. These variables are likely to contribute to the ways subjects view SQ and CS. For example, loyal customers may demonstrate a more consistent CS process than novice customers, because they are generally familiar with the product and possess well-developed expectations and perceptions. Hence the measurement could be more reliable owing to fewer variations in their responses.

As CS and SQ studies are used to formulate a company's long term commitment and investment, longitudinal studies in the area of SQ and CS could be useful for the luxury cruise industry, where the business is quite dependent on repeat customers.

Finally, it would be interesting and useful to study the service quality perceptions of cruise liners using the segmentation approach. Respondents could be segmented based on demographic factors (like gender, age, marital status, income, education level, occupation) and also by behaviouristic, geographic and psychographic factors. The findings of such a study should aim at identifying segments of the customer base which collectively have different expectations and perceptions of the service quality. This would enable cruise operators to more effectively serve the needs of the major identified segments and hence increase their competitive edge.

CHAPTER 6: STUDY TWO – SEGMENTATION OF CRUISE TRAVELLERS

6.1 Background

An essential strategy for success and survival in today's competitive business environment is to deliver quality services. (Dawkins & Reichheld, 1990; Reichheld & Sasser, 1990). This study aims to segment the customers of the leisure cruise travel industry based on their perceptions of service quality. This method of segmentation would allow cruise operators to identify and have better access to their customers through the use of target marketing. They can make use of these responses and evaluate the needs and wants of each segment more accurately and position themselves appropriately to each segment. As these market segments are easily identifiable, cruise lines can then reach their target customers more effectively.

The previous study in chapters 1 to 5 concluded that a customised instrument is more effective in measuring service quality than both the standardised instruments SERVQUAL and SERVPERF. Hence in this study the customised instrument is used as a basis for customer segmentation.

6.2 Context of the Study

Despite the region's economic woes, regional cruise lines are continuing to expand on the back of a global boom in the cruise market. Major international players in the cruise industry like Carnival, Royal Caribbean and P&O are investing heavily in some of the largest cruise ships ever built (Dahl, 1995).

Several cruise liners are turning to frequency marketing to boost passenger counts. Carnival sends issues of its Cruise magazine to all its past travellers. It also offers discounts to customers who use its affinity Visa card. Holland America woos past passengers with its "Alumni" programme, administered through a one million-past-passenger database. The average cruise traveller is 50 years old and affluent, a group that will swell in coming years as the baby boom ages. But the lines may need to find new ways to pitch cruise travelling to independent-minded boomers (Klein, 1996).

Singapore-based Star Cruises, which operates nine passenger ships in Asian waters, is fast acquiring a fleet of new superliners to rival the best in the world. Eddy Lee, CEO of Star Cruises, says that the company wants to change the popular misconception of cruise holidays as being suitable only for the middle-aged or retirees. Star Cruises has developed the regional cruising market, but is now challenged by others who believe that a traditional Asian reluctance for cruising can be overcome by more aggressive marketing of the product and the introduction of new luxury ships, purposely built for Asia (Jarett, 1997).

Three cruise lines, Carnival, Royal Caribbean and P&O carry nearly half the world's cruise passengers. The growth of the cruise market in Southeast Asia has been hampered by the lack of regional based luxury cruise liners that could run on regular fixed schedules throughout the year - with resort facilities and services catering to the increasingly sophisticated tastes and affluence of travellers in the region (Jarett, 1997).

6.3   Objectives and Scope of the Study

The objectives of this exploratory study are threefold, namely:

- to segment customers of the liner cruise travel industry on the basis of their behavioural and demographic pattern.
- to investigate whether significant differences exist in the service quality perceptions of the different identifiable segments of cruise travellers.
- to examine the managerial implications of the findings for cruise lines, especially for Star Cruises.

No previous empirical investigation available in the literature has attempted such a study of segmenting cruise travellers based on their service quality perceptions.

6.4   Need for the Study

The two strategies for enhancing a customer's value and establishing a competitive advantage which have been identified in the marketing literature are cost advantage and differentiation (Day, 1990; Kotler, 1997; Porter, 1985). A firm can differentiate its offerings through quality, innovation and brand name (Day, 1990).

The emerging empirical evidence suggests that quality affects the business performance of industrial and consumer organisations in three major ways. Firstly, quality has an impact on manufacturing and operating costs in producing both goods and services. Hard evidence suggests that increasing quality can lead to significantly lower manufacturing costs (Fine, 1986; Garvin, 1988) and increased productivity (Deming, 1982). Second there is evidence to support a relationship between price and perceived quality especially in cases where branding and product features are not significant (Gale & Klavans, 1985). Quality allows a higher price to be charged but price also provides a quality indicator under some market conditions (Philips et al., 1983). Thirdly, much of the empirical work using PIMS data base has identified a strong positive

41

association between quality improvements and market share gains (Morgan & Piercy, 1992). Empirical evidence (Buzzel & Gale, 1987) also indicates that customer's perceptions of value are more effectively changed by raising quality than by lowering cost. Quality is therefore, increasingly being recognised as the key determinant of business success and the surest way to establish a competitive advantage (Bertrand, 1989; Wulfsberg & Pulaski, 1990).

Segmentation is the act of dividing a market into distinct groups of consumers with different needs and responses (Kotler, 1997). No two consumers are alike; and because each consumer has unique needs and wants, each of them potentially represents a separate market to which an organisation can sell its goods and services. It is, however, neither practical nor realistic to tailor the product to suit the need of each individual customer. Hence, the real issue is to identify and seek out segments that respond differently and are large enough for the organisation to serve profitably.

The intended or potential beneficiaries of this research are the various cruise operators and the Port of Singapore Authority Corporation (PSA) which operates and manages the Singapore Cruise Centre.

CHAPTER 7: LITERATURE REVIEW FOR SEGMENTATION STUDY

7.1 The concept of segmentation

Market segmentation can be defined as the process of dividing a market into distinct subsets of consumers with common needs or characteristics and selecting one or more segments to target with a distinct marketing mix. Before the widespread acceptance of market segmentation, the prevailing way of doing business with consumers was through mass marketing – that is, offering the same product and marketing mix to all consumers. Wendel Smith (1956) introduced the concept of segmentation as 'based upon developments on the demand side of the market and representing a rational and more precise adjustment of product and marketing effort to consumer and user requirements.' Smith argued that there was an inherent variety in contemporary markets among users and suppliers of products. Hence market segmentation was identified as a pre-requisite for any organisation endeavouring to create products to fit customers' needs.

The strategy of segmentation allows producers to avoid head-on competition in the marketplace by differentiating their offerings, not only on the basis of price, but also through styling, packaging, promotional appeal, method of distribution and superior service. Marketers have found that the costs of consumer segmentation research, shorter production runs and differentiated promotional campaigns are usually more than offset by increased sales. In most cases, consumers readily accept the indirect cost increases for products that more closely satisfy their specific needs.

In the marketing process, the generic concept of 'target marketing' plays a very significant role (Kotler, 1997). Organisations face operational issues and challenges associated with the identification of appropriate market segments and also in the evaluation and choice between possible market segments. It is difficult for many firms to differentiate themselves to the extent of meeting individual customer needs, owing to production and cost constraints. They therefore need to consider designing services and products to meet the needs of target market segments.

Market segmentation is just the first step in a three-phase marketing strategy. After segmenting the market into homogenous clusters, the marketer then must select one or more segments to target. To accomplish this the marketer must decide on a specific product, price, channel and/or promotional appeal for each distinct segment. The third step is positioning the product so that it is perceived by each target market as satisfying that market's needs better than other competitive

43

offerings.

7.2   Segmentation Criteria

Demographic, behavioural, geographic and psychographic variables are the most commonly used forms of market segmentation for any consumer market (Kotler, 1997). Examples of each of these are shown in Table 2.1 below.

Table 7.1 : Forms of Market Segmentation

Forms of Segmentation	Examples
Demographic	Segmentation based on age, sex, family size, income, occupation, education, religion and nationality
Behavioural	Segmentation based on users' knowledge, use or response to the product or its attributes. (Include frequency of purchase, benefits sought from the purchase, user status, usage rate, loyalty status, buyer readiness stage and market focus sensitivity)
Geographic	Segmentation according to location – nations, states, cities or neighbourhood
Psychographic	Segmentation based on lifestyle or personality differences.

Demography refers to the vital and measurable statistics of a population. Demographic information is the most accessible and cost-effective way to identify a target market. Indeed, most secondary data, including census data, are expressed in demographic terms. Demographic variables reveal ongoing trends, such as shifts in age, gender and income distribution that signal business opportunities. For example, demographic studies consistently show that the 'mature-adult market" – the fifty-plus market – has a much greater proportion of disposable income than its younger counterparts. This factor alone makes consumers over 50 years old a critical market for products and services that they might buy for themselves or for their adult children.

Behavioural segmentation categorises consumers in terms of product, service, or brand usage characteristics, such as usage rate, awareness status and degree of brand loyalty. Rate of usage segmentation differentiates among heavy users, medium users, light users and non-users of a specific product, service or brand. Awareness status encompasses the notion of consumer awareness, interest level or buyer readiness. Marketers often try to identify the characteristics of their brand-loyal consumers so that they can direct their promotional efforts to people with similar characteristics in the larger population.

Geographic segmentation divides the market by location. The theory behind this strategy is that people who live in the same area share some similar needs and wants and that these needs and wants differ from those of people living in other areas.

Psychographic research, also commonly referred to lifestyle analysis is used by marketers to capture insights and to create profiles of the consumers they wish to target. Much psychographic research focuses on the measurement of activities (i.e., how the consumer or family spends time, e.g., working, vacationing, hiking), interests (the consumer's or family's preferences and priorities, e.g., home, fashion, food) and opinions (how the consumer feels about a wide variety of events and political issues, social issues, state of education and the future). In their most common form, psychographic studies use a battery of statements designed to identify relevant aspects of a consumer's personality, buying motives, interests, attitudes, beliefs and values.

7.3 Service Market Segmentation

Many aspects of segmentation and targeting for services are the same as those for manufactured goods. The main difference involves the need for compatibility in market segments. Because other customers are often present when a service is delivered, service providers must recognise the need to choose compatible segments or to ensure that incompatible segments are not receiving service at the same time. A second difference between goods and services is that service providers have a far greater ability to customise service offerings in real time than manufacturing firms have. The steps involved in segmenting and targeting services are :
✓ Identify bases for segmenting the market

✓ Develop profiles of resulting segments

✓ Develop measures of segment attractiveness

✓ Select the target segments

✓ Ensure that the target segments are compatible.

Both segmentation and customisation lead to "segments of one" or "mass customisation" – products and services designed to fit each individual's needs. The inherent characteristics of services lend themselves to customisation and support the possibility of segmenting to individual level. That is, because services are delivered to people by people, they are difficult to standardise and their outcomes and processes may be inconsistent from provider to provider, from customer to customer, and even from one time period to the next. This means that although service delivery is difficult to control and predict, it presents opportunities to customise and tailor the service in ways typically not possible for manufacturers of goods. Because the service itself is frequently delivered in "real time" by "real people" there is an opportunity for one-to-one customisation of the offering. While segments of one may be practically unrealistic in some cases, the underlying idea of crafting a customised service to fit each individual's needs fits very well with today's consumers, who demand to be treated as individuals and who want their own particular needs satisfied.

It should be noted that not all industries or individual companies offer appropriate settings for the implementation of mass customisation (Pine, Victor, & Boynton, 1993). For example, it may be very difficult to customise commodity services such as electricity or gas, and in other cases government regulations may prohibit customisation. Some companies may be too hierarchical and bureaucratic in their structure to facilitate a mass customisation strategy. And there may be cases when consumers simply do not value customisation or when they would be too confused by all the possible options. Any company that is considering a shift to mass customisation of its services will therefore have to analyse the need and feasibility of such a change.

7.4   Service Quality for Customer Segmentation

Service quality is a critical component of customer perception. In the case of pure services, service quality will be the dominant element in customers' evaluation. In cases where customer service or services are offered in combination with a physical product, service quality may also be very critical in determining customer satisfaction.

Ultimately, consumers judge the quality of services on their perceptions of the technical outcome provided and on how that outcome was delivered. For example, a restaurant customer will judge the service on his perceptions of the meal (technical outcome quality) and on how the meal was served (process quality). The existence of both process and technical quality explains why an insurance agent with superb technical skills and qualifications can fail to compete effectively with another agent who can deliver superior interpersonal quality as well. When customers cannot accurately evaluate the technical quality of a service, they form impressions of the service including its technical quality from whatever sources that exist using their own cues which may not be apparent to the provider.

The service encounter or the moment of truth is what is termed "interactive marketing". For example, a business-to-business customer who purchases a piece of equipment experiences service encounters in the sales contact, delivery, installation, billing and servicing. It is in these encounters that the customer receives a snapshot of the organisation's service quality and each encounter contributes to the customer's overall satisfaction. From the organisation's point of view, each encounter thus presents an opportunity to prove its potential as a quality service provider and to increase customer loyalty.

A number of researchers have developed industry specific scales for measuring service quality. Some of these researchers have also proposed that different scales should be designed for key customer segments even for the same service (J.J Cronin & Taylor, 1992). Genestre and Herbig (1997) examined and compared differences in service quality perceptions of three different types of retail establishments using demographic segmentation. Respondents were segmented according to gender, age, marital status, type of residence, income level and frequency of purchase. The study concluded that various segments had different service quality perceptions. They did not however, examine the marketing implications arising as a result of their findings.

Reidenbach and Minton (1991) did a similar study on the commercial banking industry. Respondents were segmented according to the length of their relationship with a specific bank. The study concluded that perceptions of bank service quality were segment specific.

Stafford (1996) segmented bank users according to demographic variables and concluded that age and gender were significant discriminators in the evaluation of service quality of banks.

Webster (1989) studied the practicality of service marketers segmenting the consumer market on the basis of its service quality expectations. Consumers' expectations were measured along various quality dimensions for three commonly purchased professional services and three non-professional services. The effect of a wide range of consumers' demographic characteristics on their service quality expectations was considered.

The articles described in the literature survey indicate that researchers have used a range of measures of service quality based on both subject perceptions and expectations. Arguments in favour of either perceptions or expectations as measurements of service quality are put forward in the next section.

7.5 Perception v/s Expectation of Service Quality

Customer expectations have been investigated in a number of settings but the most thorough treatment can be found in the customer satisfaction and dissatisfaction (CS/D) and SQ literature. While for the most part consensus exists as to their importance in evaluative models, consensus on other issues, such as the specific nature of the standard, the number of standards used, and the sources or antecedents of expectations has not yet been fully established (Zeithaml et al., 1993). In the CS/D literature, expectations are viewed as customer predictions about what is likely to happen in service/product transactions (Oliver, 1981). Oliver noted that 'it is generally agreed that expectations are consumer-defined probabilities of the occurrence of positive and negative events if the consumer engages in some behaviour'.

The multi-dimensional model of Parasuraman et al (1985; Parasuraman et al., 1988) has been widely accepted as the most comprehensive model for establishing the service quality construct (Boulding et al., 1993; J.J. Cronin & Taylor, 1994).

The conceptual model of service quality has nevertheless come under severe criticism from various service marketing researchers. Carman (1990) and Babakus and Boller (1992) argue that the five dimensions cannot be generalised across a wide spectrum of industries.

A study was done to examine the discriminant validity of SERVQUAL (Teas, 1993). In it, three important limitations of the scale were raised. Firstly, considerable variance in the respondents' interpretations of SERVQUAL's "should" or expectations measure implied that a considerable amount of the variance in service quality expectations was a result of different interpretations of the questions being asked, and not the result of different respondent attitudes and perceptions. Secondly, a relatively large number of respondents interpreted the expectations question to

48

involve a question about the attribute importance. For them, the use of the Perceptions minus Expectations (P–E) framework was inappropriate as in this situation, holding performance constant, perceived quality would increase with decreasing levels of attribute importance. Thirdly, a number of respondents interpreted the expectation measures to involve questions about 'forecast' or predicted performance levels. In this respect, the (P-E) perceived quality framework lacked discriminant validity with respect to the disconfirmed expectations component of consumer satisfaction models. The author further states that given the confusion associated with respondents' interpretation of the expectations measure and the lack of discriminant validity between the expectations measure and the other expectation concepts used in marketing, it might be useful to consider modifying the perceived service quality framework.

McDougall and Levesque (1994) used the SERVQUAL instrument to measure the service quality of retail banks. Factor analysis was performed separately on the SERVQUAL results based on the P-E scores and on SERVPERF, the unweighted perception component of SERVQUAL. Both the analysis yielded similar patterns and structures. The authors thus concluded that expectation scores do not contribute significantly to the measurement of service quality. They also noticed that the importance and expectation ratings given by the respondents were largely similar, hence suggesting that the expectation ratings were, to a certain extent, driven by importance.

Cronin and Taylor (1994) concluded through their empirical investigation that SERVPERF outperformed the unweighted SERVQUAL in predicting behavioural intentions. SERVPERF seemed to display better discriminant and nomological validity properties. Similarly Bolton and Drew (1991) have argued that customer perceptions of continuous services (e.g. telephone services) may depend solely on performance.

If both perceptions and expectations have a positive impact on customer satisfaction, then which effect should we expect to be stronger? If expectations primarily represent past quality experiences and/or non-experiential quality information, we would expect perceptions to have a greater impact for several reasons. Firstly, perceptions should be more salient and take precedence over past quality experiences in determining customer satisfaction. Actual experience with a service should outweigh other information, especially in the aggregate. Finally,

Oliver (1997) argues that transaction-specific satisfaction for ongoing consumption activities (durable goods, services, and repeatedly purchasing packaged goods) should be primarily a function of perceived performance. Expectations should be passive and have a minimal effect on satisfaction under these conditions (Bolton & Drew, 1991).

It was noticed in the first study (chapters 1 to 5) that almost all of the respondents gave a very high rating for their expectations of the various aspects of the service offerings on board a cruise ship belonging to a high performing cruise line. Also, as the survey was conducted on a brand new ship, the expectations of the respondents were naturally very high. This being the case, the 'expectation' data have very limited value when analysing responses of travellers belonging to the various segments. The 'perception' data on the other hand conjure a direct explicit sense of performance, hence the ratings given by respondents belonging to the different segments could possibly differ.

7.6   Segmentation in the Hospitality Industry

Gamble and Jones (1991) argue that the hospitality industry in general should concentrate on improving their products and services in order to create competitive advantage. They maintain that the quality of services produced is a critical factor in providing a differential advantage over competitors. In order for cruise lines to better focus their marketing efforts they might usefully segment their customers based on their perceptions of service quality. There is limited published data associated with measurement of service quality on cruise liners. However, studies using service quality as the basis of segmentation have been undertaken in similar hospitality operations such as airlines, hotels and tourism industries.

Segmentation proceeds by using two sets of variables : a grouping or segmenting variable that divides the customers and a response variable. The objective was to identify different groups of customers on the basis of their response variable.

Shaw (1994) proposed three customer groupings (based on personal characteristics and characteristics of the journey) for his study on airlines. These groupings were:

- purpose of journey (whether they are travelling for business purposes or for leisure).
- length of journey (whether they are long-haul or short-haul passengers).
- culture and origin of customers.

Response variables were the travellers' service quality perceptions of the various attributes related to airlines.

Lewis (1994) conducted surveys covering 66 attributes in six U.S. hotels. He used grouping variables of type of hotel and travel purpose and response variables of attribute importance. He concluded that attribute importance varied according to the type of hotel and the travel purpose. He also measured the gaps between U.S. hotel management and consumer expectations and perceptions. Eight gaps were identified and analysed.

Mehta and Vera (1990) surveyed 194 guests in a Singapore hotel. They segmented the market (grouping variables) based on customers' travel related behaviour, e.g. purpose of vacation, business visit, travel in a group or as an individual etc. The response variables were 26 attributes related to the selection of hotels. They concluded that the key attributes used in selecting a hotel differed in each market segment.

This research study used grouping variables based on customers' travel related behaviour and demographic characteristics.

The travel related behavioural groups were :

Travellers who had taken a cruise with the same line before, travellers who had previous experience of taking a cruise, class of travel, cabin category and travel accompaniment.

Groups based on demographics were :

Gender, marital status, age, income, education and occupation.

Response variables chosen in the study were the customers' service quality perceptions of the 40 attributes of the Customised Scale.

The literature review has revealed that although there is a well established body of work associated with service quality in hospitality operations like those in airlines, hotels and tourism industries, there is no published data available regarding service quality on cruise liners. Hence this research study associated with service quality on board cruise liners as the basis for customer segmentation should therefore endeavour to close this obvious gap in the literature.

51

CHAPTER 8 : DATA ANALYSIS FOR SEGMENTATION STUDY

8.1 Sample Profile

Out of the 300 questionnaires distributed, 202 were returned. However, 12 of these had to be discarded due to incompleteness. The overall response rate (67.3%) was considered satisfactory given the length of the questionnaire.

Table 8.1 : Response Rate

Questionnaires	Frequency	Percent
Given Out	300	100%
Returned	202	67.3%
Discarded	12	4.0%
Usable	190	63.3%

8.2 Segmentation By Previous Experience

Table 8.2 : Respondents by Previous Experience of Star Cruises

Type of Traveller	Frequency	Percent
Experienced	103	54.2 %
First time traveller	87	45.8 %
Total	190	100 %

Table 8.3 : Tests of Mean Differences in Perception Scores by Previous StarCruise Experience

Type Of Traveller	Factor 1 Liner Service Personnel			Factor 2 On-board Services			Factor 3 Operational Features			Factor 4 Supplementary Services			Overall Service Quality		
	Mean	Std. Dev	Sig. (p)	Mean	Std. Dev	Sig. (p)	Mean	Std. Dev	Sig. (p)	Mean	Std. Dev	Sig. (p)	Mean	Std. Dev	Sig. (p)
Experienced	5.44	0.74	0.15	5.00	0.86	0.73	6.00	0.69	0.21	5.51	1.28	0.49	5.57	0.88	0.00*
First-time	5.59	0.68		4.95	0.80		6.11	0.51		5.41	0.63		5.98	0.74	

* Significant at 5% level

52

While the mean perception scores for overall service quality differed, there were no significant differences across all the four factors between the two groups. First timers perceived the overall service quality of Star Cruises significantly higher than experienced travellers. This was possibly because experienced travellers could have compared the overall service with what they had previously experienced on other cruise liners belonging to Star Cruises.

8.3   Segmentation By Previous Liner Experience

Table 8.4 : Respondents by Previous Cruise Experience

Type of Traveller	Frequency	Percent
Experienced	76	40.0 %
Inexperienced	114	60.0 %
Total	190	100 %

Table 8.5 : Tests of Mean Differences in Perception Scores By Previous Cruise Experience

Type Of Traveller	Factor 1 Liner Service Personnel			Factor 2 On-board Services			Factor 3 Operational Features			Factor 4 Supplementary Services			Overall Service Quality		
	Mean	Std. Dev	Sig. (p)	Mean	Std. Dev	Sig. (p)	Mean	Std. Dev	Sig. (p)	Mean	Std. Dev	Sig. (p)	Mean	Std. Dev	Sig. (p)
Experienced	5.48	0.71	0.70	4.96	0.86	0.78	6.15	0.60	0.04*	5.55	0.67	0.34	5.72	0.81	0.59
In- Experienced	5.52	0.72		4.99	0.82		5.98	0.62		5.41	1.22		5.78	0.87	

*   Significant at 5% level

ANOVA revealed that there was a significant difference in the mean perception scores of Factor 3 (Operational Features). In order to investigate further, an item-by-item analysis of this factor was performed as shown in *Appendix 2.*

53

The only significant differences in the mean perception scores of experienced and in-experienced travellers were in items 68 and 35. Experienced travellers could possibly have seen better photo gallery and check-in/check-out facilities on board other cruise liners that they had previously sailed on.

8.4 Segmentation by Class of Travel

Table 8.6 : Respondents by Class of Travel

Class of Travel	Frequency	Percent
Stateroom	127	67.2 %
Stateroom with balcony	57	30.2 %
Suite	5	2.6 %
Total	189	100 %

Table 8.7 : Tests of Mean Differences in Perception Scores By Class of Travel

Class Of Travel	Factor 1 Liner Service Personnel			Factor 2 On-board Services			Factor 3 Operational Features			Factor 4 Supplementary Services			Overall Service Quality		
	Mean	Std. Dev	Sig. (p)	Mean	Std. Dev	Sig. (p)	Mean	Std. Dev	Sig. (p)	Mean	Std. Dev	Sig. (p)	Mean	Std. Dev	Sig. (p)
Stateroom	5.56	0.74		5.06	0.86		6.07	0.65		5.50	1.17		5.77	0.91	
Stateroom with balcony	5.39	0.65	0.30	4.83	0.75	0.19	5.98	0.54	0.61	5.38	0.67	0.76	5.77	0.70	0.62
Suite	5.44	0.61		4.70	0.71		6.11	0.51		5.55	0.97		5.40	0.54	

There were no significant differences in the mean perception scores of passengers travelling in different classes. This was possible because majority of the service quality attributes did not relate to the living environment. Further research is necessary to know the differences between the characteristics of travellers using these three classes.

8.5   Segmentation by Cabin Category

Table 8.8 : Respondents by Cabin Category

Class of Travel	Frequency	Percent
Twin	90	47.6 %
Triple	39	20.6 %
Quad	60	31.8 %
Total	189	100 %

Table 8.9 : Tests of Mean Differences in Perception Scores By Cabin Category

Category Of Cabin	Factor 1 Liner Service Personnel			Factor 2 On-board Services			Factor 3 Operational Features			Factor 4 Supplementary Services			Overall Service Quality		
	Mean	Std. Dev	Sig. (p)	Mean	Std. Dev	Sig. (p)	Mean	Std. Dev	Sig. (p)	Mean	Std. Dev	Sig. (p)	Mean	Std. Dev	Sig. (p)
Twin	5.65	0.66		5.05	0.83		6.22	0.49		5.68	1.30		5.87	0.68	
Triple	5.47	0.64	* 0.02	4.84	0.81	0.41	5.98	0.57	* 0.00	5.36	0.47	* 0.01	5.69	0.97	0.19
Quad	5.31	0.81		4.95	0.84		5.83	0.74		5.20	0.77		5.63	0.95	

*   significant at 5% level

ANOVA revealed that there were significant differences in the mean perception scores for Factors 1, 3 and 4. However, as there were 3 categories of cabins, Multiple Comparisons were performed using Scheffes Post-Hoc tests. Results of these tests are shown in *Appendix 3.* The conclusion was that perception scores from travellers in Twin-sharing cabins were significantly higher (for Factors 1, 3 and 4) than those for travellers in Quad-sharing cabins. The perception scores of travellers in Triple-sharing cabins were in the middle of the other two, not significantly different from either. Tukey HSD Post-Hoc Test was also performed to confirm this result. The output is also shown in *Appendix 3.* In order to investigate further, an item-by-item analysis of Factors 1,3 and 4 was performed using ANOVA. The results of these analysis are shown in *Appendix 2* which can be summarised as follows :

For Factor 1, items 8, 17, 6, 16 and 5 contributed most towards significantly higher mean perception scores of passengers in the Twin-sharing cabins as compared to those in the Quad-sharing cabins.

For Factor 3, all the items except items 2 and 68 contributed towards significantly higher mean perception scores of passengers in Twin-sharing cabins as compared to those in the Quad-sharing cabins.

For Factor 4, items 56, 62, 64 and 55 contributed the most towards significantly higher mean perception scores of passengers in Twin-sharing cabins as compared to those in the Quad-sharing cabins.

8.6 Segmentation by Travel Accompaniment

Table 8.10 : Respondents by Travel Accompaniment

Travel Accompaniment	Frequency	Percent
Alone	2	1 %
With Family	109	57.4 %
In a Group	79	41.6 %
Total	190	100 %

As there were only 2 respondents who were travelling alone (1%) this group of travellers had been intentionally left out of the analysis.

Table 8.11 : Tests of Mean Differences in Perception Scores by Travel Accompaniment

Travel Accompani-ment	Factor 1 Liner Service Personnel			Factor 2 On-board Services			Factor 3 Operational Features			Factor 4 Supplementary Services			Overall Service Quality		
	Mean	Std. Dev	Sig. (p)	Mean	Std. Dev	Sig. (p)	Mean	Std. Dev	Sig. (p)	Mean	Std. Dev	Sig. (p)	Mean	Std. Dev	Sig. (p)
With Family	5.52	0.78		4.86	0.86		6.12	0.61		5.43	0.74		5.74	0.86	
			0.31			* 0.02			* 0.03			0.27			0.45
In a Group	5.46	0.62		5.11	0.75		5.93	0.60		5.48	1.34		5.77	0.81	

* significant at 5% level

ANOVA revealed that there were significant differences in the perception scores of Factors 2 and 3.   In order to investigate further, an item-by-item analysis of these Factors was performed as shown in *Appendix 2*. The summary of this analysis was as follows :

For Factor 2, items 36, 69 and 53 contributed significantly to the difference in the mean perception scores between respondents travelling with their families and those travelling in a group with friends or relatives. Those in a group scored higher on items 36 and 69, whereas those travelling with families scored higher on item 53.

For Factor 3, items 30, 74 and 23 contributed significantly to the difference in the mean perception scores between respondents travelling with their families and those travelling in a group with friends or relatives. Group travellers scored lower on all the three items.

8.7 Segmentation By Gender

Table 8.12: Respondents by Gender

Gender	Frequency	Percent
Male	108	56.8 %
Female	82	43.2 %
Total	190	100 %

Table 8.13 : Tests of Mean Differences in Perception Scores By Gender

Gender	Factor 1 Liner Service Personnel			Factor 2 On-board Services			Factor 3 Operational Features			Factor 4 Supplementary Services			Overall Service Quality		
	Mean	Std. Dev	Sig. (p)	Mean	Std. Dev	Sig. (p)	Mean	Std. Dev	Sig. (p)	Mean	Std. Dev	Sig. (p)	Mean	Std. Dev	Sig. (p)
Male	5.55	0.69		4.99	0.88		6.06	0.63		5.38	0.70		5.71	0.91	
Female	5.47	0.74	0.47	4.97	0.77	0.84	6.03	0.59	0.68	5.59	1.36	0.16	5.83	0.75	0.32

* significant at 5% level

From the above Table 8.13 it can be seen that there were no significant differences in the perception scores across all the 4 factors and also for the Overall Service Quality between males and females.

8.8 Segmentation By Marital Status

Table 8.14: Respondents by Marital Status

Marital Status	Frequency	Percent
Single	66	34.7 %
Married	110	57.9%
Others	14	7.4 %
Total	190	100 %

Since the number of respondents in the 'Others' category was very small (7.4%), this category had been intentionally eliminated from further analysis.

Table 8.15: Tests of Mean Differences in Perception Scores By Marital Status

Marital Status	Factor 1 Liner Service Personnel			Factor 2 On-board Services			Factor 3 Operational Features			Factor 4 Supplementary Services			Overall Service Quality		
	Mean	Std. Dev	Sig. (p)	Mean	Std. Dev	Sig. (p)	Mean	Std. Dev	Sig. (p)	Mean	Std. Dev	Sig. (p)	Mean	Std. Dev	Sig. (p)
Single	5.48	0.62		4.96	0.75		5.90	0.63	*	5.50	0.61		5.82	0.79	
Married	5.52	0.80	0.93	5.02	0.90	0.83	6.09	0.59	0.03	5.45	1.28	0.97	5.73	0.87	0.89

*   significant at 5% level

ANOVA revealed that there were significant differences in the mean perception scores for Factor 3. In order to investigate further, an item-by-item analysis of this Factor was performed as shown in *Appendix 2.*

The significant differences in the mean perception scores of Single and Married travellers were in items 25, 71, 74 and 23. Singles rated all the significantly different items of the Operational Features of Star Cruises lower than the ratings given by Married travellers.

8.9 Segmentation By Age

Table 8.16 : Respondents by Age

Age Group	Frequency	Percent
Below 25	34	17.9 %
25 to 45	112	58.9%
Above 45	44	23.2 %
Total	190	100 %

Table 8.17 : Tests of Mean Differences in Perception Scores By Age

Age Group	Factor 1 Liner Service Personnel			Factor 2 On-board Services			Factor 3 Operational Features			Factor 4 Supplementary Services			Overall Service Quality		
	Mean	Std. Dev	Sig. (p)	Mean	Std. Dev	Sig. (p)	Mean	Std. Dev	Sig. (p)	Mean	Std. Dev	Sig. (p)	Mean	Std. Dev	Sig. (p)
Below 25 years	5.48	0.71		5.06	0.75		5.82	0.67		5.48	0.68		5.79	0.81	
25 to 45 years	5.46	0.70	0.29	4.95	0.82	0.79	6.08	0.62	* 0.05	5.51	1.23	0.70	5.76	0.81	0.97
Above 45 years	5.66	0.75		4.99	0.91		6.15	0.54		5.35	0.67		5.75	0.96	

* significant at 5% level

ANOVA revealed that there were significant differences in the mean perception scores for Factor 3 (Table 8.17 above). However, as there were 3 categories of Age groups, Multiple Comparisons were performed using Scheffes Post-Hoc tests. Results of these tests are shown in *Appendix 3.* The conclusion was that perception scores given by those in the 'Below 25 years' group were significantly different than those given by the 'Above 45 years' group. The mean perception scores of those in the '25 to 45 years' group were in the middle of the other two, not significantly different from either. Tukey HSD Post-Hoc Test was also performed to confirm this result. The output is also shown in *Appendix 4.* In order to investigate further, an item-by-item analysis of Factors 3 was performed using ANOVA. The results of these analysis are shown in *Appendix 2*.

The only significant differences in the mean perception scores of travellers below 25 years old and those above 45 years old were in items 25, 71 and 23. Younger travellers rated all the items of the Operational Features of Star Cruises lower than the ratings given by the older age group of travellers.

8.10   Segmentation By Personal Income

Table 8.18: Respondents by Personal Income

Personal Income	Frequency	Percent
No income	47	24.7 %
Less than $ 5000 p.m.	91	47.9 %
Above $ 5000 p.m.	52	27.4 %
Total	190	100 %

Although income has been an important variable for distinguishing market segments, a major problem with segmenting the market on the basis of income alone is that income simply indicates the ability (or inability) to pay for a product.   For this reason, marketers often combine income with some other demographic variable(s) to define their target markets more accurately. For example, high income can be combined with age to identify the important affluent elderly segment. It can also be combined with age and occupational status to produce the so-called yuppie segment, a sought-after subgroup of the baby boomer market.

The 'no income' group in this study which made up 24.7% of the respondents, included housewives, students, those enlisted in the army (NS men), unemployed persons and retirees.

Table 8.19 : Tests of Mean Differences in Perception Scores By Personal Income

Personal Income	Factor 1 Liner Service Personnel			Factor 2 On-board Services			Factor 3 Operational Features			Factor 4 Supplementary Services			Overall Service Quality		
	Mean	Std. Dev	Sig. (p)	Mean	Std. Dev	Sig. (p)	Mean	Std. Dev	Sig. (p)	Mean	Std. Dev	Sig. (p)	Mean	Std. Dev	Sig. (p)
No income	5.45	0.92		5.03	0.91		5.84	0.77		5.31	0.88		5.62	1.01	
Less than $ 5000 p..m.	5.52	0.69	0.80	4.99	0.76	0.72	6.12	0.53	* 0.03	5.66	1.23	0. 06	5.88	0.71	0.14
Above $ 5000 p.m.	5.54	0.55		4.90	0.89		6.10	0.57		5.25	0.68		5.67	0.88	

*   significant at 5% level

ANOVA revealed that there were significant differences in the mean perception scores for Factor 3. However, as there were 3 groups of Personal Income, Multiple Comparisons were performed using Scheffes Post-Hoc tests. Results of these tests are shown in *Appendix 5*. The conclusion was that perception scores given by respondents in the 'No Income' group were significantly different from those given by the 'Less than $ 5000 p.m.' group. The mean perception scores of those in the 'Above $ 5000 p.m.' group were in the middle of the other two, not significantly different from either. Tukey HSD Post-Hoc Test was also performed to confirm this result. This output is also shown in *Appendix 5*. In order to investigate further, an item-by-item analysis of Factor 3 was performed using ANOVA. The results of these analysis are shown in *Appendix 2*.

Significant differences existed between the mean perception scores of travellers who had no income (retirees, students etc) and those whose income was below $ 5000 per month in items 30, 25, 1, 74 and 35. The former group had lower ratings on all the items as compared to the later group.

8.11 Segmentation By Level of Education

Table 8.20 : Respondents by Level of Education

Type of Education	Frequency	Percent
Secondary School	45	23.7 %
A-Levels / Polytechnic	75	39.5 %
University & Above	70	36.8 %
Total	190	100 %

Table 8.21 : Tests of Mean Differences in Perception Scores By Level of Education

Education Level	Factor 1 Liner Service Personnel			Factor 2 On-board Services			Factor 3 Operational Features			Factor 4 Supplementary Services			Overall Service Quality		
	Mean	Std. Dev	Sig. (p)	Mean	Std. Dev	Sig. (p)	Mean	Std. Dev	Sig. (p)	Mean	Std. Dev	Sig. (p)	Mean	Std. Dev	Sig. (p)
Secondary School	5.48	0.91		5.22	0.96		5.81	0.78		5.56	1.78		5.64	1.00	
A-Levels / Polytechnic	5.42	0.64	0.31	4.88	0.80	0.08	6.05	0.59	* 0.01	5.41	0.67	0. 74	5.74	0.79	0.41
University & Above	5.60	0.65		4.92	0.75		6.19	0.47		5.46	0.63		5.85	0.78	

*   significant at 5% level

ANOVA revealed that there were significant differences in the mean perception scores for Factor 3 (Table 4.21). However, as there were 3 Levels of Education, Multiple Comparisons were performed using Scheffes Post-Hoc tests. Results of these tests are shown in *Appendix 6*. The conclusion was that perception scores given by respondents with a Secondary education were significantly different from those given by respondents with a University education. The mean perception scores of those with A-Levels or Polytechnic Education were in the middle of the other two, not significantly different from either. Tukey HSD Post-Hoc Test was also performed to confirm this result. The output is also shown in *Appendix 6*. In order to investigate further, an item-by-item analysis of Factor 3 was performed using

ANOVA. The results of these analysis are shown in *Appendix 2.*

Significant differences existed between the mean perception scores of respondents who had a Secondary education and those whose had a University education in items 30, 25, 74, 23 and 68. Respondents who had only a Secondary education rated all the items lower than those who had a University education.

8.11 Segmentation by Type of Occupation

Table 8.22 : Respondents by Type of Occupation

Type of Occupation	Frequency	Percent
Not working	44	23.2 %
Clerical / Production	19	10.0 %
Managerial	93	48.9 %
Own Business	34	17.9 %
Total	190	100 %

Table 8.23 : Tests of Mean Differences in Perception Scores By Type of Occupation

Occupation Type	Factor 1 Liner Service Personnel			Factor 2 On-board Services			Factor 3 Operational Features			Factor 4 Supplementary Services			Overall Service Quality		
	Mean	Std. Dev	Sig. (p)	Mean	Std. Dev	Sig. (p)	Mean	Std. Dev	Sig. (p)	Mean	Std. Dev	Sig. (p)	Mean	Std. Dev	Sig. (p)
Not Working	5.43	0.93		5.02	0.91		5.83	0.79		5.32	0.91		5.59	1.04	
Clerical / Production	5.28	0.59	0.25	4.72	0.49	0.17	5.78	0.61	* 0.01	5.67	2.48	0. 56	5.73	0.81	0.44
Managerial	5.54	0.58		4.92	0.79		6.20	0.49		5.53	0.62		5.83	0.75	
Own Business	5.65	0.78		5.20	0.93		6.06	0.57		5.40	0.74		5.82	0.82	

*   significant at 5% level

ANOVA revealed that there were significant differences in the mean perception scores for Factor 3. However, as there were 4 categories of Occupation, Multiple Comparisons were performed using Scheffes Post-Hoc tests. Results of these tests are shown in *Appendix 7*. The conclusion was that perception scores given by respondents who were not working were significantly different from those given by respondents who were in managerial positions. Tukey HSD Post-Hoc Test was also performed to confirm this result. The output is also shown in *Appendix 7*. In order to investigate further, an item-by-item analysis of Factor 3 was performed using ANOVA. The results of these analysis are shown in *Appendix 2*.

Significant differences existed between the mean perception scores of respondents who were unemployed and those whose were in managerial positions in items 30, 25, 1, 74, 23 and 35. Respondents holding managerial positions gave higher scores to all the 9 items of Factor 3.

8.12 Differences in satisfaction levels

Table 8.24 : Tests of Mean Differences in ratings of Customer Satisfaction

Demographics & Travel Behaviour	Group 1		Group 2		Group 3		Group 4		ANOVA Sig *	Post-Hoc Test
	Mean	Std. Dev	Mean	Std. Dev	Mean	Std. Dev	Mean	Std. Dev		
Gender	5.62	0.81	5.65	0.87					0.86	
Marital Status	5.66	0.78	5.63	0.88	5.57	0.75			0.86	
Age	5.64	0.84	5.59	0.81	5.75	0.89			0.56	
Income	5.61	1.01	5.65	0.72	5.63	0.86			0.97	
Education	5.62	0.91	5.67	0.81	5.71	0.81			0.60	
Occupation	5.61	1.03	5.52	0.77	5.63	0.77			0.82	
Cruise experience	5.51	0.91	5.72	0.78					0.09	
Class of Travel	5.66	0.89	5.61	0.73	5.40	0.55			0.75	
Cabin Category	5.77	0.77	5.53	0.85	5.50	0.89			0.10	
Journey Accomp.	6.50	0.71	5.55	0.90	5.73	0.72			0.11	

* Significant at 1 % level

ANOVA revealed that there were no significant differences in the ratings of Customer

64

Satisfaction between all the categories of respondents except for some weak evidence ($p<0.1$) of the following two which were based on their travel behaviour :

i)   previous cruise experience

ii)   cabin category

Respondents who had previously travelled on cruises were less satisfied overall as compared to those who were first timers on this cruise. It is possible that respondents with previous cruise experience compared the service quality of Star Cruises with what they may have experienced on some of the world's best cruise lines.

Also respondents travelling in Quad-sharing cabins rated their overall satisfaction lower than those travelling in other types of cabins.

The demographic variables of Nationality and Race which were obtained using Section C of the questionnaire, were intentionally left out of the segmentation analysis. Firstly, a very large majority of the respondents were Singaporeans (80%). This was justifiably so because the cruise used Singapore as the home port for embarking and disembarking passengers. The 15% of foreigners included Malaysians, Britons, Australians and a few other nationalities. It would be reasonable to expect Malaysian respondents to have quite similar views concerning service quality on board cruise liners as their Singaporean counterparts. Secondly, 90% of the Singaporean and Malaysian respondents were Chinese (Race). This is owing to the fact that people of Chinese origin are generally more affluent both in Singapore and in Malaysia.

CHAPTER 9: IMPLICATIONS AND RECOMMENDATIONS OF THE SEGMENTATION STUDY

9.1 Conclusion

The strategy of segmentation allows cruise operators to avoid head-on competition in the market place by differentiating their offerings, not only on the basis of price, but also through packaging, promotional appeal and superior service. In the marketing process, the generic concept of 'target marketing' plays a very significant role (Kotler, 1997). This study aims to segment cruise travellers based on their perceptions of service quality. The customised instrument which proved (in the first study) to be more effective than SERVQUAL and SERVPERF in measuring service quality on board cruise liners was used as a basis of customer segmentation.

Table 9.1 on the next page summarises items which were found to be significantly different among the various groups of cruise travellers.

Table 9.1 : Summary of Differences for all items across Segments

Segment Factors/ Items	Experience of Star Cruise (Experience /First-timers)	Previous Cruise Experience (Experience /Inexperien-ced)	Cabin Category (Twin/ Quad)	Travel Accomp-animent (With Family/ Group)	Marital Status (Single/ Marr-ied)	Age (Below 25/ Above 45)	Perso-nal Income (No income/ Less than $ 5000)	Educat-ion (Second-ary/ Univer-sity)	Occu-Pation (Not working/ Manag-ers)
Factor 1 Items			Quad lower on 8,17,6,16 and 5.						
Factor 2 Items				Family lower on 36, 69. Group lower on 53					
Factor 3 Items		Experien-ced lower on 68, 35	Quad lower on 30,25,71, 74,23 and 35.	Group lower on 30,74,2 and 3.	Singles lower on 25,71, 23	Below 25 lower on 25,71,2 and 3	No income lower on 30,25,1,7 4and 35	Secondary lower on 30,25,74 23,68.	Not working lower on 30,25,1, 74,23,3 and 5
Factor 4 Items			Quad lower on 56,62,64 and 55.						
Overall Service Quality	Experien-ced lower								

Respondents who had previously travelled on cruise liners belonging to Star Cruises rated the overall service quality significantly lower than those who were travelling with Star Cruises for

67

the very first time.

The mean perception scores of experienced cruise travellers on items related to photo gallery and check-in/check-out facilities was significantly lower than those who were travelling on a cruise for the first time.

Travellers occupying Quad sharing cabins gave significantly lower scores for several items of Liner Service Personnel, Operational Features and Supplementary Services as compared to those travelling in other types of cabins.

Those travelling in a group gave significantly lower scores for the item "snacks in between meals" and also for four items of Operational Features as compared to those travelling with their families. It is possible that the expectations of those travelling in a group could have been higher.

Singles gave significantly lower scores for four items of Operational features as compared to those given by married respondents.

Younger travellers gave significantly lower scores on three items of Operational features as compared to those given by respondents over 45 years old. The three items had all to do with the living environment like comfortable ships, good cabin cleaning facilities and spacious rooms.

Travellers who had no income (students, homemakers and retirees included) gave significantly lower scores as compared those whose income was less than $ 5000 per month, on four items belonging to Operational Features.

Travellers with a lower educational background (Secondary school) gave significantly lower scores on five items belonging to Operational Features as compared to those who had a Post-graduate education.

Lastly those who were not working (students, homemakers and retirees included) gave significantly lower scores as compared to those who had managerial jobs for seven items of Operational Features.

The above summary indicates that differences in service quality do exist between various groupings. This finding is in line with similar studies undertaken by Lewis (1994) in six U.S. Hotels and also by Mehta and Vera (1990) who surveyed 194 guests in a Singapore hotel.

9.2 Implications

Firms that use market segmentation can pursue a concentrated marketing strategy or a differentiated marketing strategy. Once Star Cruises has identified its most promising market segments, it must decide whether to target one segment or several. The premise behind market segmentation is that each targeted segment receives a specially designed marketing mix. Targeting several segments using individual marketing mixes is called differentiated marketing; targeting just one segment with a unique marketing mix is called concentrated marketing.

From the analysis it is evident that passengers travelling in Quad-sharing cabins have rated a number of items lower than those travelling in Twin-sharing cabins. This should be a cause of concern to Star Cruises, and the items they should attend to are:

- Meet needs of passengers correctly upon first request.
- Have employees who are competent in performing their duties.
- Handle complaints from passengers promptly.
- Have courteous and polite employees.
- Have employees who meet passengers' requests in a reasonable time.
- Have convenient ticket reservation system.
- Receive strong support from its travel agents.
- Have hassle-free pre-boarding security screenings.
- Handle reservation services efficiently.

It is possible that Star Cruises has inadvertently provided a higher quality of service to those travelling in Twin and Triple sharing cabins, probably at the expense of those travelling in Quad-sharing cabins. Although it is true that Quad-sharing passengers pay lower fares than others, there is no reason why they should not be entitled to receive services from competent liner personnel who are courteous and polite to them and who handle their complaints promptly.

Thought should be given about the standards people are using to make these judgements of quality, i.e. the perceptions might be lower because they have formed higher expectations. This may have some marketing implications for Star Cruises. It can manage service perceptions by improving the level of performance or by endeavouring to manage customer expectations, i.e. by reducing the gap between Perceptions and Expectations (P–E) as suggested by Parasuraman et al (1988). Such a move will have positive effects on overall customer satisfaction and on post-purchase behavioural consequences such as customer loyalty, word-of-mouth and recommendation to others.

It is evident from Table 9.1 that Factor 3 (Operational Features) is the dominant factor which is rated lower by the following segments of travellers :

Experienced, Quad-sharing, travelling in a group, singles, below 25 years of age, students and retirees, secondary school educated and homemaker/student.

The sort of uniform pattern that has emerged across the above segments, and items which have contributed towards this weakness are :

- Have clean and well maintained ships.
- Have ships which are comfortable to sail on.
- Have good cabin maintenance and cleaning facilities.
- Have good photo gallery facilities.
- Have fast check-in and check-out facilities.

The management of Star Cruises will have to take corrective action to rectify the perceptions of their clients belonging to the segments mentioned above.

One glaring area which Star Cruises will need to tackle is the implications of the differences in overall quality perception between experienced and inexperienced travellers. It may need to formulate a marketing strategy to correct this situation, as experienced travellers contribute significantly to post-purchase behavioural consequences such as customer loyalty, word-of-mouth and recommendation to others.

Star Cruises will have to attend to the needs of passengers travelling with families with special regard to the following items :

- Provide a variety of beverages.
- Have good arrangements for viewing the ship's bridge and other places of interest.

A well-designed customer database is also critical. Star Cruises needs to know who its current customers are (names, addresses, phone numbers, etc.), what their buying behaviour is, the revenue they generate, the related costs to serve them, their preferences and relevant segmentation information (e.g. demographics, lifestyle, usage patterns). Star Cruises needs to focus on relationship marketing, the benefits of customer segmentation and the importance of identifying the right market segment(s) for relationship building. Once it has carefully identified its market segments and developed quality services, it can use some specific tactics like financial bonds, social bonds, customisation bonds and structural bonds to accomplish the goal of retaining its customers (Zeithaml & Bitner, 2000).

Financial Bonds : cruise travellers can be tied to the company primarily through financial incentives like frequent traveller programmes. Such programmes which have been proliferated in the airline industry, are not difficult to initiate and they frequently result in at least short term profit gains. Also, by linking cruise mileage points earned to usage of other firm's services (e.g. hotel chains) customers can enjoy even greater financial benefits in exchange for their loyalty.

Social Bonds : cruise travellers should be viewed as 'clients' and not as nameless faces. They should be treated as individuals whose needs and wants the cruise line seeks to understand. Services should be customised to fit individual needs and marketers should find ways of staying in touch with their customers. Such ways include maintaining good relations with clients to assess their changing needs, providing personal touches like cards and gifts, and sharing personal information with them. While social bonds alone may not tie the customer permanently to the firm, they are much more difficult for competitors to imitate than are price incentives.

Customisation Bonds : two commonly used terms which fit within this approach are mass customisation and customer intimacy. Both of these strategies suggest that customer loyalty can be encouraged through intimate knowledge of individual customers and through the development of 'one-to-one' solutions that fit the individual customer's needs. Mass customisation has been defined as the use of flexible processes and organisational structures to produce varied and often individually customised products and services at the price of standardised, mass-produced alternatives. It provides customers, through little effort on their part, with tailored services to fit their individual needs.

Structural Bonds : often such bonds are created by providing customised services to the client that are technology based and serve to make the customer more productive. One way would be for cruise operators to tie their main booking agents closer to them by providing them with free on-line booking computers which store addresses and data about past cruise travellers. However, the potential downside to this arrangement is that the booking agents may fear that tying themselves close to one cruise operator may not allow them to take advantage of potential price savings from other cruise operators in the future.

Through the use of segmentation, Star Cruises can isolate the items in each segment where the customers reported low ratings. Identifying the root of these weaknesses can give Star Cruises an edge over its competitors in its quest for a greater market share. It can perform a thorough investigation and seek appropriate remedial action to improve the perception ratings of its customers belonging to particular segments.

Although the data analysis and findings in Chapter 8 have highlighted certain segments as having significant differences in the mean perception score of some items, the majority of the items have not been featured in our discussion. Hence it is useful to look at the overall mean perception scores of all respondents as a group. Tables 9.2 and 9.3 show the top ten and bottom ten items, rated according to their mean perception scores.

Table 9.2 : Top ten items in relation to Mean Perception Score of All Items

Item No.	Description of Item	Perception	
		Mean	Std. Dev
48	Are punctual in departure and arrival time	6.60	1.23
30	Have clean and well maintained ships	6.52	0.69
74	Have ships which behave well whilst sailing	6.36	0.94
2	Have attractive ambience and décor on ships	6.31	0.80
25	Have ships which are comfortable to sail on	6.30	1.02
1	Have a modern fleet of ships	6.29	0.88
71	Have good cabin maintenance and cleaning facilities	6.24	0.86
16	Have courteous and polite employees	6.08	1.13
12	Have employees who are always willing to help	5.78	0.84
3	Have employees with professional appearance	5.78	0.99

Table 9.3 : Bottom ten items in relation to Mean Perception Score of All Items

Item No.	Description of Item	Perception	
		Mean	Std. Dev
63	Offer frequent traveller programmes	3.63	1.79
69	Have good arrangements for viewing the ship's bridge	4.60	1.54
34	Provide food that caters to the needs of different passengers	4.69	1.29
24	Serve delicious and tasty food	4.71	1.24
40	Provide a variety of main courses of food	4.85	1.15
36	Provide a variety of beverages on the cruise	4.93	1.37
7	Have employees who rarely make mistakes	4.94	1.03
18	Have employees who pay individualised attention to passengers	5.05	1.02
31	Serve food that is fresh	5.10	1.21
73	Have good shows and entertainment for adults	5.12	1.12

Star Cruises should endeavour to maintain the high quality of services rendered in Table 9.2. Additionally they should take remedial action to improve the perception ratings on items listed in Table 9.3. Of particular concern are items related to Food & Beverage. They should effectively cater to the differing needs of passengers, eg. vegetarian and sugar-free meals. They also need to serve delicious and tasty food and provide a variety of main courses for the passengers to choose from.

However before putting effort into improving the worst ten items, Star Cruises would need to know more about the effects of these variables on behavioural intentions. That is, if these things are not very important in relation to the likely repurchase or word-of-mouth recommendation, then it might not be as important to spend a lot of effort in improving performance. This of course is the purpose of the third research study.

9.3 Limitations and Suggestions for Future Research

Although the overall results of this study are quite encouraging, their implications may be limited by several considerations.

Firstly the primary data collection for this study was undertaken on a very modern cruise liner. There could be substantial differences in the perception of travellers sailing on older cruise liners. These would possibly be in the areas of tangibles like brand new facilities and interior décor.

Secondly, the length of the questionnaire might have made it a tiring task for some respondents to fill in. This may have resulted in some respondents misrepresenting their actual perceptions of the various attributes of service quality.

Thirdly, majority of the respondents were Singaporean Chinese. Possibly some of them may not have been well versed in understanding the English language. These respondents would have preferred the questionnaire to be written in the Chinese language.

Fourthly, the findings of this survey could have been supplemented by the findings of in-depth interviews conducted on board the liner with travellers who were randomly selected.

Fifthly, perception scores used for this study are generally related to the organisation and may not necessarily be typical of the industry. Hence any recommendations which are made as a result of the analysis would be more applicable to the organisation, which in this case is Star Cruises.

Sixthly, the relationship between service quality and consumer behavioural intentions (e.g.

73

customer loyalty) should be explored. This will enable Star Cruises to allocate its marketing resources towards retaining its existing customers. In fact, it is estimated that it costs five times as much to attract a new customer as it does to retain a current customer (Desatnick, 1988). Understanding the relationship between service quality and consumer behavioural intentions would therefore be useful in demonstrating the impact of service improvements on the profits of Star Cruises.

Finally, psychographic variables like lifestyle or personality differences of respondents could possibly be used to undertake segmentation studies of service quality on board cruise liners.

CHAPTER 10: STUDY THREE - LOYALTY AND FUTURE PATRONAGE OF CRUISE TRAVELLERS

10.1 Service Quality, Customer Satisfaction and Behavioural Consequences

The service marketing literature in the 1990s has witnessed a resurgent interest in examining the financial and strategic consequences of service improvement measures such as service quality and customer satisfaction (Zeithaml, Berry, & Parasuraman, 1996). Two streams of research emerged to justify the financial accountability of investing on improving service quality and customer satisfaction. The first employed analytical and mathematical tools to directly calculate the return on service improvements, and linked measures of customer satisfaction with company performance (E. W. Anderson & Fornell, 1994; Zahorik & Rust, 1993). Aggregate measures across consumers and companies were used in this school of research. The second stream, on the other hand, tried to understand the service quality and financial consequence relationship from the consumer's point of view and resorted to a behavioural perspective e.g. (Zeithaml et al., 1996). Surprisingly, only a few studies have focused on the impact of customer satisfaction on behavioural responses. Our understanding of the behavioural consequences of customer satisfaction remains considerably on the easily accepted intuition that superior customer satisfaction will drive favourable consumer responses. However, several aspects need to be addressed to fully elicit the effects of customer satisfaction in differing circumstances.

The common assumption is that service quality leads to satisfied customers (E. W. Anderson & Fornell, 1994; Reidenbach & Minton, 1991; Woodside, Frey, & Daly, 1989). For example, a customer who is leaving a restaurant or hotel is asked if he was satisfied with the service he received. If he answers "no", then we tend to assume that the service quality was poor. Customer satisfaction refers to either a discrete, time-limited event or the entire time the service is experienced. Service-encounter satisfaction is how much a customer likes or dislikes an actual service encounter. Overall service satisfaction is the customer's feeling of satisfaction or dissatisfaction based on all the customer's experiences with the service organisation. Bitner and Hubbert (1994) argued that the constructs of service encounter satisfaction and overall service satisfaction differed from each other and from service quality.

Studies of consumer behaviour emphasise customer satisfaction as the core of the postpurchase period (Westbrook & Oliver, 1991). Because customer satisfaction is an antecedent of repeat purchases and favourable word-of-mouth publicity (Fornell, Johnson, Anderson, Cha, & Gryant,

1996), this concept is essential to marketers. Customer satisfaction serves as an exit barrier, thereby helping the firm to retain its customers (Halstead & Page, 1992). As service quality and customer satisfaction relate to retention of customers at the aggregate level, it would be useful to determine their impact on particular behaviours that signal whether customers remain with or defect from a company.

10.2 Context of the Study

This study is related to the luxury cruise industry. Despite the economic woes in South East Asia, regional cruise lines are continuing to expand on the back of a global boom in the cruise market. Major international players in this industry are investing heavily in some of the largest cruise ships ever built. Singapore-based Star Cruises embarked on a rapid fleet expansion programme in 1997, and now has 9 cruise liners plying in the Asian region. The world's second largest cruise operator, Royal Caribbean International, is looking to base one of its ships here next year. Its president, Mr Jack Williams remarked, "Asia has always been high on our list of priorities. Now that the economic crisis seems to be behind the Asian markets, our purpose is to understand and evaluate the market potential" (Times, 2000). In December 1998, Singapore welcomed its millionth passenger at the Singapore Cruise Centre after seven years of intensive promotion.

Unlike land-based resorts and tours, a cruise includes almost all of the costs involved in travelling. The ticket price covers meals, entertainment, sightseeing and often tips. "When you buy a cruise, you get it all" (Murphy, 1996). Value has helped cruise lines attract many first-time passengers, particularly young families of baby-boom generation parents. A cruise has a predictable impact on the family budget and it allows families with children to explore exotic locations and to enjoy a host of family activities like karaoke and magic shows. Cruise operators tend to focus on reusing the experienced passenger more often instead of reaching the first-time cruiser. " Its easier and cheaper harvest fields you've planted than to plant new fields" (Murphy, 1996).

10.3 Objectives and scope of the Study

The aims of this exploratory study are to investigate the impact of service quality on overall satisfaction and behavioural consequences of customers of the leisure cruise industry in Singapore. More specifically, the objectives of this research are :

a) to investigate the relationship between the various dimensions of service quality and overall customer satisfaction of cruise travellers

76

b) to investigate the relationship between the various dimensions of service quality and the post-purchase behavioural intentions of cruise travellers.

c) To investigate the relationship between customer satisfaction and behavioural intentions of cruise travellers.

d) to categorise cruise travellers into groups based on their post-purchase behavioural intentions and to investigate whether significant differences exist among different categories.

e) to examine the marketing implications of the findings for cruise lines, especially for Star Cruises.

10.4 Contribution of the research

The research findings derived from this study will endeavour to close the gap in the service quality literature associated with travel especially with leisure cruise travel. Empirical research has identified a positive association between service quality improvements and market share (Buzzel & Wiersema, 1991). Increasing service quality has a potentially enormous impact on profitability, through reducing an organisation's operating cost and improving its market position. Service quality is increasingly being offered as the strategy for organisations to position themselves in the marketplace (S. W. Brown & Swartz, 1989; J.J Cronin & Taylor, 1992; Zeithaml et al., 1993).

As a result of this study leisure cruise operators will be better able to :

• determine the service quality factors affecting overall customer satisfaction of cruise travellers.

• know the impact of service quality on their customers' behavioural intentions, which in turn affects their bottom-line profits.

• allocate their resources for service improvements.

• identify the differences in customer satisfaction and behavioural intentions between different groups that may exist in their customer base and utilise these differences in formulating service quality strategies.

CHAPTER 11- LITERATURE REVIEW OF THE LOYALTY STUDY

11.1 Customer Perceptions

It is important to know how customers perceive services, how they assess whether they have experienced quality services and whether they are satisfied. Perceptions are always considered relative to expectations and because expectations are dynamic, perceptions may also shift over time – from person to person and from culture to culture. What is considered quality service or the things that satisfy customers today may be different tomorrow. Customers perceive services in terms of the quality of the service and how satisfied they are overall with their experiences. The customer-oriented terms of 'Quality' and 'Satisfaction' have been the focus of attention for executives and researchers for a long time. Today companies recognise the fact that they can compete more effectively by distinguishing themselves with respect to service quality and improved customer satisfaction.

Although the terms 'Satisfaction' and 'Quality' are interchangeably used by practitioners and writers, researchers have attempted to be more precise about the meanings and measurement of the two concepts. There is growing consensus that the two concepts are fundamentally different in terms of their underlying causes and outcomes (Parasuraman et al., 1994). While they have certain things in common, Satisfaction is generally viewed as a broader concept while Service Quality assessment focuses specifically on dimensions of service. Based on this view, perceived service quality is a component of customer satisfaction. Service Quality is a focused evaluation that reflects the customer's perception of specific dimensions of service : responsiveness, reliability, tangibles, assurance and empathy. Satisfaction, on the other hand, is more inclusive : it is influenced by perceptions of service quality, product quality and price as well as situational and personal factors.

11.2 Customer Satisfaction

Satisfaction is the customers' evaluation of a product or service in terms of whether that product or service has met their needs and expectations. Failure to meet needs and expectations is assumed to result in dissatisfaction with the product or service. There are two conceptualisations of customer satisfaction in the current literature : *transaction-specific* and *cumulative* (E. W. Anderson & Fornell, 1994; Boulding et al., 1993), with the latter being adopted in this study. From the transaction-specific perspective, consumers make post-choice evaluation about their satisfaction with a specific purchase experience (Oliver, 1997). Cumulative customer satisfaction, in contrast, reflects the overall evaluation based on the total purchase and consumption experience with a service over time (Fornell et al., 1996).

The transaction-specific conceptualisation of customer satisfaction is meaningful for those who need diagnostic information about a particular service encounter to monitor and improve service offerings. However, cumulative customer satisfaction is more relevant to managers interested in building long-term relationship with a stable customer base, because it provides a more fundamental indicator of consumers' global assessment and appreciation of the firm's past, current and future performance (E. W. Anderson & Fornell, 1994). Additionally, occasional favourable experience is not sufficient to keep customers loyal in today's highly competitive market. Cumulative customer satisfaction is relatively more stable than the transaction-specific one an thus is a better basis for consumers' ongoing judgement and evaluation, especially for infrequently purchased services such as cruises. Only those service providers who can consistently meet customers' needs and desires can successfully retain their customers and can achieve their financial objectives.

With the cumulative perspective of customer satisfaction being adopted in this study, the dominant "disconfirmation of expectation" paradigm seems conceptually inappropriate. This paradigm states that consumers make pre-purchase expectations, evaluate service performance, compare the evaluations with their expectations, and determine whether and how they are satisfied with this specific experience based on the extent to which their evaluations exceed expectations (Johnson et al., 1995). The comparison between service performance and expectation takes place across experiences and should be more compatible with transaction-specific satisfaction. In contrast, cumulative customer satisfaction is the global evaluation of past experiences with the company, in which consumers directly evaluate performance instead of comparing it with expectations.

Given the diversity of needs of cruise travellers, customer satisfaction should have multiple components. The subjective judgement of one component of customer satisfaction may be independent of that of other components, because different components are supposed to address different consumer needs. Hence cruise travellers may employ different standards and/or evaluative processes when they make judgement on different components of satisfaction. It can be argued that they make not only overall satisfaction judgement, but also individual satisfaction judgement on particular components of customer satisfaction.

It is imperative to distinguish between the antecedents and the components of customer satisfaction. Antecedents of satisfaction are constructs that directly or indirectly affect satisfaction evaluation. They are independent of, though causally related to customer satisfaction. They can be some form of consumers' subjective judgement as well as some objective factors such as price. In comparison, components of customer satisfaction are different kinds of satisfaction judgements associated with different needs supposed to be satisfied. The components can be operationally regarded as the dimensions of overall customer satisfaction. Studies on antecedents of satisfaction address the question "how customer satisfaction is created and what determines the level of satisfaction", whereas components of satisfaction help to answer the question "with what needs are customers satisfied ?".

11.3 Service Quality

Service quality is a critical component of customer perceptions. In the case of pure services, service quality will be the dominant element in customers' evaluation. In cases where customer service or services are offered in combination with a physical product, service quality may also be very critical in determining customer satisfaction.

Consumers judge the quality of services on their perception of the technical outcome provided and how that outcome was delivered. A person who dines in a restaurant will judge the service on his perceptions of the meal (technical outcome quality) and on how the meal was served and how the employees interacted with him (process quality).

Research suggests that customers do not perceive quality as a unidimensional concept, i.e. customers' assessment of quality include perceptions of multiple factors (Zeithaml et al., 1993). For example, it has been suggested that the following eight dimensions of quality are applied to all goods and services : performance, features, reliability, conformance, durability, serviceability, aesthetics and perceived quality (roughly equivalent to prestige) (Garvin, 1988).

Possibly the most widely reported determinants of service quality are conceptualised in the SERVQUAL model developed by Parasuraman et al (1988). They found that consumers consider five dimensions in their assessment of service quality. These dimensions are :

- Reliability : Ability to perform the promised service dependably and accurately.

- Responsiveness : Willingness to help customers and provide prompt services.
- Assurance : Employees' knowledge and courtesy and their ability to inspire trust and confidence.
- Empathy : Caring, individualised attention given to customers.
- Tangibles : Appearance of physical facilities, equipment, personnel and written materials.

On the basis of exploratory and quantitative research, these five dimensions were found relevant for banking, insurance, appliance repair and maintenance, securities brokerage, long-distance telephone service and automobile repair service.

Although SERVQUAL has been widely accepted as the most comprehensive model for establishing the service quality construct, it has nevertheless been criticised by several service marketing researchers. Carman (1990) and Babakus and Boller (1992) argue that the five dimensions cannot be generalised across a wide spectrum of industries. Vandamme and Leunis (1992) caution against using SERVQUAL to service categories which have little elements in common with services already investigated with this instrument.

The first study in Chapters 1 to 5 which was aimed at measuring the service quality in the leisure cruise industry compared the relative effectiveness of SERVQUAL, SERVPERF and a customised instrument. It was evident from the findings of this study that the customised instrument which was specially developed for the leisure cruise industry was more effective in measuring service quality than both SERVQUAL and SERVPERF. The customised instrument yielded four factors, which were : Liner Service Personnel, On-board Services, Operational Features and Supplementary Services.

The present study uses both the scales, SERVQUAL and customised, so as to provide greater confidence and more reliable answers to the question of relationship between service quality, overall customer satisfaction and behavioural intentions of cruise travellers.

11.4   Service Quality and Behavioural Intentions

As it is difficult to predict and understand behaviours, it has been suggested that people will generally act in accordance with their predisposing intentions (Ajzen & Fishbein, 1980). This predisposition or attitude is seen as a determining factor in a consumer's behaviour towards the offering as future need arises. Behavioural intentions generally fall into two categories, namely, favourable and unfavourable. Favourable behavioural intentions include customers being loyal, praising the firm, expressing preference for the firm, increasing the volume of their purchases and agreeably paying a price premium. Unfavourable behavioural intentions on the other hand, include customers complaining to their friends and external agencies, switching to competitors or decreasing the amount of business with the company (Berry et al., 1996).

An intent to behave is a result of experience with a service or information deemed relevant by the consumer about that service (Headly & Miller, 1993). Consumers' perceived service quality is found to have a strong influence on their behavioural intentions. Woodside et al (1989) used a single basic repurchase intent measure to associate the measurement of quality in the context of hospital stays. They found that service quality does have a strong relationship with consumers' intentions to return to the same hospital provider. Reidenbach and Smallwood (1990) found a positive and strongly correlated relationship between the patient's overall perception of service quality, their satisfaction of the treatment and their willingness to recommend the hospital. Berry et al (1996) also found a positive and significant relationship between customers' perceptions of service quality and their willingness to recommend the company. Headly and Miller (1993) found a significant relationship between perceived service quality and customer's intent to repurchase, recommend, compliment, complain, switch and not use a certain medical care service.

Studies have found relationships between service quality and more specific behavioural intentions. In one study involving university students, strong links between service quality and other behavioural intentions of strategic importance to a university were found, including saying positive things about the school, planning to contribute money to the class pledge upon graduation, and planning to recommend the school to employers as a place from which to recruit (Boulding et al., 1993). Another comprehensive study examined a battery comprising of 13 specific behavioural intentions likely to result from perceived service quality. The overall measure was significantly correlated with customer perceptions of service quality (Zeithaml et al., 1996). Lastly a study quantitatively assessed the relationship between the level of service quality and willingness to purchase at AT&T. Of AT&T's customers who rated the company's overall quality as excellent, more than 90 percent expressed willingness to purchase from AT & T again. For customers rating the service as good, fair, or poor, the percentages decreased to 60, 17 and 0 percent, respectively. According to these data, willingness to repurchase increased at a steeper rate (i.e. by 43 percent) as the service quality rating improved from fair to good than when it went from poor to fair (17 percent) or from good to excellent (30 percent)(Gale, 1994).

11.5 Customer Loyalty

Customer loyalty is characterised by a high degree of satisfaction with a firm and is reflected by a combination of attitudes and behaviours (Prus & Brandt, 1995). These attitudes include: intentions to buy again and/or buy additional products and services from the same company, willingness to recommend the company to others and finally commitment to the company demonstrated by a resistance to switching to a competitor. The behaviours include : repeat purchasing of products and services, purchasing more and different products or services from the same company and finally recommending the company to others.

Firms can adopt two types of strategies to improve sales and market share. These are offensive and defensive strategies. Offensive strategies are described as those designed to obtain additional customers, encourage brand switching and increase purchase frequency. On the other hand, defensive strategies are described as those concerned with reducing customer exit and brand switching. Thus defensive marketing is concerned with maximising customer retention by protecting products and markets from competitors (Fornell & Wernerfelt, 1988). The effects of service quality on customer retention has been termed as the defensive impact of service quality.

The cost of generating a new customer can be much higher than the cost of retaining an existing customer. This is because attracting new customers involves advertising, promotion and sales costs. Moreover, new customers are often unprofitable in the short-term period. Loyal customers are more likely than short-term customers to buy additional services, spread favourable word-of-mouth communication, pay a higher price and be served more efficiently owing to the experience curve effect (Reichheld & Sasser, 1990).

In this study, customer loyalty is measured by four behavioural intentions, which are :
 i)   Say positive things about the cruise line to other people.
 ii) Recommend the cruise line to someone who seeks advice.

iii) Encourage friends and relatives to travel on cruises operated by the cruise line.

iv) Consider the cruise line as the first choice to travel on a cruise.

11.6 Service Quality, Customer Retention and Profits.

Although it is important to understand the relationship between overall service quality and profitability, it is perhaps more useful to managers to identify specific drivers of service quality that most relate to profitability. Doing so will help firms understand what aspects of service quality to change to influence the relationship, and therefore where to invest resources. Most of the studies in this area have examined the aspects of service (for example, empathy, responsiveness and tangibles) on overall service quality, customer satisfaction and purchase intentions rather than on financial outcomes such as retention or profitability.

Traditionally, organisations have measured their performance on the basis of financial indicators such as profit, sales and return on investment. This short-term approach leads companies to emphasise financial returns to the exclusion of other performance indicators.

The costs of attracting new customers should be lower for firms that achieve a high level of customer satisfaction (Fornell et al., 1996). For example, satisfied customers are reputedly more likely to engage in positive word of mouth, and less likely to engage in damaging negative word of mouth for the firm (Reichheld & Sasser, 1990).

An increase in customer satisfaction should improve the overall reputation of the firm. An enhanced reputation can assist in introducing new products by providing instant awareness and lowering the buyer's risk of trial (Robertson & Gatignon, 1986). According to Aaker (1992) customer satisfaction should play an important role in building other important assets for a firm, such as brand equity.

Although delivering quality service is considered an essential strategy for success and survival in today's competitive environment (Reichheld & Sasser, 1990; Zeithaml et al., 1993), some managers are hesitant to invest in improving their services unless they obtain tangible evidence of the financial returns. It is true that although 90% of large U.S. corporations have some form of quality-improvement programmes, several recent studies reveal that many of these programmes are unsuccessful (Zahorik & Rust, 1993). This goes to prove that service quality is not necessarily a guarantee of profitability. There are however, several studies like the PIMS (Profit Impact of Market Strategy) which have found strong positive relationships between return on investment (ROI) and reported quality levels, and between quality and market share growth (Zahorik & Rust, 1993). The central chain of events that leads from quality to profits is summarised in Figure 11.1 below.

Figure 11.1 : Chain of events that leads from quality to profits

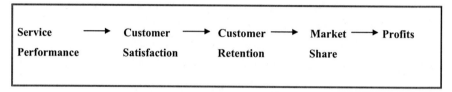

The above chain of events focuses on customer retention and does not include three sources of profits generated by quality improvement, namely, cost reductions due to increased efficiency, the attraction of new customers resulting from positive word-of-mouth and the ability to charge higher prices (Zahorik & Rust, 1993).

This concept is supported by Buzzel and Wiersema (1991) who found that companies which offer superior service achieve higher-than-normal market share growth.

Zeithaml et al (1996) developed a conceptual model of the impact of service quality on particular behaviours that signal whether customers remain with or defect from a company. Additionally, to study the practicality of service improvement efforts, they examined changes in the quality-intentions link at different service levels relative to customers' expectations. This is shown in the figure 11.2 on the next page.

Figure 11.2 : The Behavioural and Financial Consequences of Service Quality

Adapted from : Zeithaml, Berry and Parasuraman (1996), The Behavioural Consequences of Service Quality

The literature review reveals that overall customer satisfaction and service quality are likely to be critical factors in providing a differential advantage for a cruise line over its competitors. Hence cruise lines must primarily identify the criteria and dimensions which affect overall satisfaction of their customers. There is hardly any published data regarding overall customer satisfaction and post-purchase behavioural consequences associated with hospitality operations like airlines, hotels, tourism industries and cruise liners. Findings of this research paper will therefore endeavour to close this obvious gap in the literature.

11.7 Formulation of Hypotheses

Based on the literature review the following hypotheses were formulated :

$H_0 1$: there is no significant relationship between the service quality measures of SERVQUAL and customer satisfaction of cruise travellers.

$H_0 2$: there is no significant relationship between the service quality measures of the customised scale and customer satisfaction of cruise travellers.

$H_0 3$: there is no significant relationship between the service quality measures of SERVQUAL and the behavioural intentions of cruise travellers.

$H_0 4$: there is no significant relationship between the service quality measures of the customised scale and the behavioural intentions of cruise travellers.

CHAPTER 12 : METHODOLOGY AND DATA ANALYSIS

12.1 Development of Questionnaire

The two instruments used in this study were the 22-item SERVQUAL and a customised instrument.

The 22-item SERVQUAL scale developed by Parasuraman et al (1988) was used in its entirety. However, amendments in the wording and phrasing of some of the items were made to reflect the special nature of services produced by Star Cruises. Each of the 22 items had to be rated on a 7 point Likert scale for both the expectation and perception scores.

Relevant literature and focus group techniques were used to develop the customised instrument. Two focus group interviews were held with people who had travelled on Star Cruises and one focus group interview was held with the marketing personnel of Star Cruises. Each of these focus groups consisted of five to six persons. The groups were asked to discuss the attributes of services on cruise liners which they considered important and essential. Schiffan and Kanuk (1997) recommend usage of the focus group technique in the early stages of attitude research.

A 75-item customised instrument was developed as an outcome of the focus group interviews. 22 of these items closely matched with those already included in the SERVQUAL.

It was decided to obtain expectation and perception ratings on a 7 point Likert scale for all of the 75 items of the customised instrument.

12.2 Design of the Questionnaire

The final questionnaire as shown in *Appendix 1* consisted of six sections as follows :

Section A was designed to obtain information about respondents' travelling behaviour.

Section B consisted of the 75-item customised scale. Against each of these items, respondents were required to rate (on a 7 point Likert scale) their expectations of a high performing cruise line and also their perceptions of services provided by Star Cruises. SERVQUAL ratings were obtained from the first 22 items of the customised instrument. This was deliberately done so as to avoid making the questionnaire too lengthy.

Section C which is a part of SERVQUAL required the respondent to allocate a total of 100 points among the five dimensions of tangibility, reliability, responsiveness, assurance and empathy.

Section D was designed to obtain information about the demographic characteristics of respondents such as gender, nationality, marital status, age, income and educational level and occupation.

Section E was used to assess the feelings of respondents after they had been on the cruise. In other words, it was used to assess the post-purchase behavioural intentions of cruise travellers.

Section F was designed to obtain the overall customer satisfaction of cruise travellers.

12.3 Pilot Study

Seven persons who had previously travelled on cruise liners were involved in the pilot test which was conducted to detect and clarify any mistakes and ambiguity in the questionnaire. A small number of typing errors and ambiguous statements were rectified. Also, initially the expectation and perception statements were typed out on separate pages. This made the questionnaire rather lengthy and tedious for the respondent to complete. It was thus decided to present both the expectation and perception statements together on a single page, thus considerably reducing the length of the final questionnaire.

12.4 Sampling Plan

It was decided to use a non-probability sampling method (convenience sampling) owing to time and cost factors. Also a sample size of approximately 300 seemed adequate as this number was consistent with previous studies undertaken on service quality in the hospitality area.

It was noted that meaningful responses could be elicited from travellers who had recently experienced the cruise. Hence, four trained interviewers (with the permission of Star Cruises) joined a 4 day cruise on the megaship "Superstar Leo".

12.5 Collection of Data

The "Superstar Leo" sailed out of Singapore Port on a 4 day cruise with approximately 2000 passengers on board. The trained interviewers distributed survey questionnaires to the passengers on the second day of the cruise. A detailed explanation was given to each of the respondents regarding the purpose of the survey and also where the completed questionnaire had to be deposited. As a small incentive to complete the questionnaire each of the respondents were given a keychain as a souvenir from Star Cruises. A total of 300 questionnaires were distributed.

Although this number seems small in relation to the total number of passengers on the cruise, it must be noted that majority of them were travelling either with their families (57.4%) or in a group (41.6%).

A box was placed at the reception counter for respondents to drop the completed questionnaires prior to their departure. Before the cruise ended at Singapore on the 4th day, an announcement was made on the public address system gently reminding passengers about the survey questionnaires.

12.5 Factor Analysis performed previously

In the first study, Factor Analysis was performed on the 75 attributes of the customised instrument. After subjecting the data to a varimax rotation, 40 attributes were retained under four factors. These factors which explained 50.6% of the total variances were :

i)   Liner service personnel

ii)   On-board services

iii)   Operational features

iv)   Supplementary services

The 4 factors and the attributes associated with each of them are shown in Table 12.1 on the next page.

Table 12.1 : Factors derived from the customised scale

Factor	Attributes	Factor Ldg	EXPECTATION		PERCEPTION	
			Mean	Std.Dev	Mean	Std.Dev
Factor 1	Meet needs of passengers correctly upon first request	0.80	6.14	0.79	5.34	0.96
	Have employees who provide prompt services	0.74	6.53	0.62	5.67	0.93
	Carry out passengers' requests or instructions without error	0.74	6.03	0.81	5.33	0.90
	Have employees who are competent in performing their duties	0.73	6.71	0.62	5.73	1.07
	Handle complaints from passengers promptly	0.72	6.44	0.65	5.49	0.99
	Have courteous and polite employees	0.68	6.66	0.65	6.08	1.13
	Have employees with professional appearance	0.66	6.57	0.64	5.78	0.99
	Have employees who are sympathetic and reassuring when passengers encounter problems	0.63	6.39	0.66	5.34	1.01
	Have employees who always find time to meet passengers' requests	0.62	6.35	0.67	5.50	0.88
	Have employees who pay individualised attention to passengers	0.60	5.92	0.97	5.05	1.02
	Have employees who are always willing to help	0.59	6.58	0.65	5.78	0.84
	Have employees who rarely make mistakes	0.59	5.63	1.03	4.94	1.03
	Have employees who meet passengers' requests in a reasonable time	0.56	6.35	0.67	5.59	0.91
Factor 2	Provide food that caters to needs of different passengers (e.g. vegetarian food, halal food, baby food, low fat/ calories, diabetic diet etc)	0.71	6.54	0.85	4.69	1.29
	Serve food that is fresh	0.71	6.76	0.58	5.10	1.21
	Provide a variety of beverages on the cruise	0.68	6.19	0.94	4.93	1.37
	Provide a variety of main courses of food that passengers can choose from	0.66	6.29	0.78	4.85	1.15
	Have good arrangements for viewing the ship's bridge and other places of interest on the ship	0.64	6.41	0.80	4.60	1.54
	Serve delicious and tasty food	0.61	6.60	0.68	4.71	1.24
	Have good shows and entertainment for adults	0.57	6.52	0.84	5.12	1.12
	Have good Casino and Jackpot facilities	0.55	4.78	1.79	5.41	1.11
	Serve adequate snacks in between meals	0.53	5.95	1.00	5.22	1.12
	Have good arrangements for shore excursions	0.50	6.38	0.81	5.14	1.20
Factor 3	Have clean and well maintained ships	0.78	6.58	0.69	6.52	0.69
	Have ships which are comfortable to sail on	0.66	6.64	0.67	6.30	1.02
	Have a modern fleet of ships	0.65	6.43	0.77	6.29	0.88
	Have good cabin maintenance and cleaning facilities	0.56	6.57	0.71	6.24	0.86
	Have attractive ambience and decor on their ships	0.56	6.61	0.59	6.31	0.80
	Have ships which behave well whilst sailing, thus reducing chances of sea-sickness	0.56	6.54	0.71	6.36	0.94
	Have spacious rooms to sleep and relax comfortably	0.48	6.38	0.87	5.55	1.17
	Have good photo gallery facilities	0.41	5.37	1.29	5.38	1.21
	Have fast and efficient check-in and check-out facilities	0.39	6.43	0.72	5.48	1.23
Factor 4	Have convenient ticket reservation system	0.79	6.76	1.17	5.61	1.03
	Receive strong support from its travel agents	0.68	6.15	0.87	5.59	1.29
	Have hassle-free pre-boarding security screenings	0.67	6.23	0.79	5.61	0.99
	Handle reservation services efficiently	0.60	6.34	0.67	5.59	1.05
	Inform travellers of any delays to the cruise departures well in advance	0.51	6.59	3.62	5.72	0.91
	Have proper lost baggage procedures	0.50	6.26	0.78	5.39	0.88
	Offer frequent traveller programmes	0.46	5.89	1.00	3.63	1.79
	Are punctual in departure and arrival time	0.25	6.42	0.80	6.60	5.23

The Kaiser-Meyer-Olkin (KMO) value obtained for the customised scale was 0.891. this figure is considered to be extremely good for a factor analysis model (Kaiser, 1974).

It was decided to use both the SERVQUAL and Customised Scales in this study so as to provide greater confidence and more reliable answers to the question of relationships between service quality, customer satisfaction and behavioural intentions.

12.6 Statistical Tools Used

Reliability analysis was performed to measure the reliability of both SERVQUAL and the customised instrument. A commonly used reliability coefficient, Cronbach's Alpha was used to indicate the internal consistency of the two scales. As a rule-of-thumb, values of Cronbach's Alpha above 0.7 would be sufficient evidence that a scale is of acceptable reliability.

To detect for the existence of any possible correlation, Pearson's correlation coefficient was used to measure the strength and direction of linear association between the explanatory variables.

Multiple regression was used to test the first four hypotheses. The dependent variables used were overall customer satisfaction scores and behavioural intention mean scores, while the explanatory variables were the dimensions of factors associated with each of the two instruments. The corresponding Coefficient of Determination, R^2, found from the regressions were used to compare the explanatory power of each instrument. R^2 refers to the proportion (per cent) of the total variation in the dependent variable (overall service quality) that is explained by the set of explanatory variables (service quality dimensions). Effectively, R^2 measures the goodness of fit of a model.

To counter the problems of artificially high R^2 caused by few observations in the sample or more independent variables included in the multiple regression equation given a fixed number of observations (overfitting), the adjusted R^2 incorporates the effect of including independent variables in a multiple regression equation. It is an important summary statistic to evaluate how well the multiple regression model fits the data (Watson et al., 1993).

One-way analysis of variance (ANOVA) was used to determine if there were any significant difference in the means of perception ratings of the four factors and the overall service quality, between groups of a particular segment.

In ANOVA an F statistic was used to assess the overall differences in the response variable between the groups formed by the independent variable. Examination of the group means was used to assess the relative standing of each group on the dependent measure. While the F statistic test assesses the null hypothesis of equal means, it does not address the question of which means are different. For example, in a three-group situation, all three groups may differ significantly, or two may be equal but differ from the third. To assess these differences, either planned comparisons or Post Hoc tests can be used. In a situation such as this where it was required to make pairwise comparison of all means, it was appropriate to use Post Hoc testing procedures.

Among the more common Post Hoc procedures are Scheffe's test, Tukey's honestly significant difference (HSD) method, Tukey's extension of the Fisher least significant difference (LSD) approach, Duncan's multiple-range and finally the Newman-Kuels test. Each method identifies which comparisons among groups (e.g. group 1 versus groups 2 and 3) have significant differences. These procedures were used to test combinations of groups, thus simplifying the interpretative process.

Because the Post Hoc tests must examine all possible combinations, the power of any individual test is rather low. The five tests mentioned above have been contrasted for power. The conclusions are that Scheffe's test is the most conservative with respect to Type I error. The remaining tests are ranked in this order : Tukey HSD, Tukey LSD, Newman-Kuels and Duncan.

The basis of the order of the tests that were used was from highest power to lowest power. Hence it was decided to use Tukey HSD test which is the most powerful alongwith the conservative Scheffe's test for comparison purposes.

12.7 Sample Profile

Out of the 300 questionnaires distributed, 202 were returned. However, 12 of these had to be discarded due to incompleteness. The overall response rate (67.3%) was considered satisfactory as the questionnaire was quite lengthy.

Table 12.2 : RESPONSE RATE

Questionnaires	Frequency	Percent
Given Out	300	100%
Returned	202	67.3%
Discarded	12	4.0%

The demographic profile and travel behaviour of respondents is shown in *Appendix 2*. Males made up 56.8% and females 43.2% of the respondents. Majority of the respondents were married (57.6%), whilst singles (34.7%) included children of parents who were travelling on board. The largest category of age group was that of travellers between 35 and 44 years (30%) followed by those between 25 and 34 years (28.9%). Respondents who did not earn any income (24.7%) were housewives, retirees and students. 27.4% of the respondents were degree holders whilst 22.6% had diplomas from Polytechnics. 24.7% of the respondents held managerial positions closely followed by those who were not working, including students (23.2%). 40% of the respondents had travelled on a cruise before this one. Majority of the respondents travelled in staterooms (67.2%) and in twin cabins (47.6%). Lastly majority of them travelled with their families (57.4%) while 41.6% travelled in a group.

12.8 SERVQUAL Dimension Scores

The mean perception scores (weighted and unweighted) of the five dimensions of SERVQUAL scale were computed. Weights were obtained from the importance ratings allocated by respondents in Section C of the survey questionnaire which is shown in *Appendix 1*. These scores are shown in the Table below

.

Table 12.3 : Mean perceptions scores for the five dimensions of SERVQUAL

Dimension	Unweighted Mean	Weighted Mean	Std Dev of Weighted Mean
Assurance	5.83	5.87	0.78
Tangibles	5.72	5.70	0.61
Responsiveness	5.64	6.68	0.76
Reliability	5.35	5.37	0.78
Empathy	5.25	5.22	0.74

Additionally, a new variable was created from the 22 items of the SERVQUAL scale (arithmetic

94

mean) to represent an average rating of the scale. This was done to obtain an overall measure of the service across all of the items in the SERVQUAL scale.

Reliability Analysis of SERVQUAL Dimensions

Results of the reliability analysis are shown in Table below.

Table 12.4 : Results of reliability analysis of SERVQUAL dimensions (Perception scores)

Dimension	Items Included	Cronbach Alpha
Tangibles	1. Modern fleet of ships 2. Attractive ambience and décor on ships 3. Employees who have a professional appearance 4. Charge low fares for the cruises	0.72
Reliability	1. Employees who meet passengers' requests in a reasonable time 2. Handle complaints from passengers promptly 3. Employees who rarely make mistakes 4. Meet needs of passengers correctly upon first request 5. Carry out passengers' requests or instructions without error	0.76
Responsiveness	1. Employees who are concerned, responsive and attentive to passengers' needs 2. Employees who provide prompt services 3. Employees who are always willing to help 4. Employees who always find time to meet passengers' needs	0.83
Assurance	1. Employees who instill confidence 2. Make passengers feel safe 3. Courteous and polite employees 4. Employees who are competent in performing their duties	0.87
Empathy	1. Employees who pay individualised attention to passengers 2. Convenient arrival and departure times 3. Employees who understand the needs of different nationalities 4. Employees who are sympathetic and reassuring to passengers 5. Meet the needs of special passengers like elderly and infants	0.78

The results in Table 12.4 show that the coefficient alpha values were consistently high across the five service quality dimensions. Since in all cases, the reliability coefficients exceeded Nunnally and Bernstein (1994) criteria of minimum acceptable reliability of 0.7, it could be concluded that there was a high internal consistency among items within each SERVQUAL dimension. Additionally, the overall SERVQUAL scale was assessed using Cronbach's alpha and the computed reliability coefficient was 0.85 which is again within acceptable limits.

12.9 Customised Scale

Factor Scores

Table 12.5 : Factor scores of the Customised Scale

Factor (Dimension)		Customised Instrument	
		Mean	Standard Deviation
Factor 3	Operational Features	6.05	0.62
Factor 1	Liner Service Personnel	5.51	0.72
Factor 4	Supplementary Services	5.47	1.04
Factor 2	On-board Services	4.98	0.83

The above mean scores were derived from the perception ratings of all items included in the factors. The highest mean rating of 6.05 was given to 'Operational Features' whereas 'On-board Services' were rated the lowest at 4.98. The data could not be weighted as the factors were generated after data collection.

Reliability analysis of the Customised Scale

Table 12.6 : Reliability analysis of the Customised Scale

Factor (Dimension)	Cronbach Alpha (α)
Liner Service Personnel	0.93
On-board Services	0.86
Operational Features	0.79
Supplementary Services	0.52

The results show that the coefficient alpha values were consistently high across the four factors of the customised scale. Since these coefficients exceeded Nunnally and Bernstein's (1994) criteria of minimum acceptable reliability of 0.7, it could be conclude that there was a high degree of internal consistency among the items within each factor.

Overall Customer Satisfaction

The mean score obtained for Overall Customer Satisfaction (on a scale of 1 to 7 as shown in Section F of the survey questionnaire in *Appendix 1*) was 5.64 and the Std. deviation was 0.84.

12.10 Behavioural Intentions of Cruise Travellers

Section E of the survey questionnaire (*Appendix 1*) was designed to obtain information about the behavioural intentions of cruise travellers. In order to make this information more meaningful the four questions were regrouped as follows :

1. Word of mouth (represented by question number one)
2. Recommendation to others (represented by question numbers two and three)
3. Future patronage (represented by question number four)

The means of these three variables are presented in Table 4.6 below :

Table 12.7 : Mean scores of behavioural intentions of cruise travellers

Name of Group	Mean Score	Std Dev.
1. Word of Mouth	5.94	0.78
2. Recommendations to others	5.84 *	0.84
3. Future Patronage	5.42	1.12

* arithmetic average of two items

Behavioural Intentions and Overall Customer Satisfaction

Pearson's Correlation was used to compare the mean scores of the three variables of cruise travellers' post-purchase behavioural intentions with the overall customer satisfaction score. The results are shown in the Table below.

Table 12.8 : Correlation Coefficients of the three variables of Behavioural Intentions and Overall Customer Satisfaction

Correlation Coefficient	Word of Mouth	Recommendations	Future Patronage	Overall customer satisfaction
Word of Mouth	1.00	0.81	0.56	0.72
Recommendations	-	1.00	0.72	0.71
Future Patronage	-	-	1.00	0.58
Overall Customer Satisfaction	-	-	-	1.00

r > 0.196 for significance at 5% level ; r > 0.234 for significance at 1% level

97

Overall satisfaction had a relatively strong relationship with all the three variables of behavioural intention. This finding is in line with the findings of similar studies undertaken in the area of post-purchase behavioural intentions. Also, the relationship between overall satisfaction was higher with 'Word of mouth' and 'Recommendation' than with 'Future Patronage'. Presumably this was because some travellers even though they are satisfied and happy to tell others, might consider a cruise to be a one-off experience, something they are not likely to want to do again.

12.11 SERVQUAL, CS and Behavioural Intentions

Correlations

Pearson's Correlation was used to investigate the relationship of SERVQUAL dimensions with customer satisfaction and behavioural intentions. This is shown in the Table below.

Table 12.9: Correlation Coefficients (r) of SERVQUAL with Customer Satisfaction and Behavioural Intentions

SERVQUAL Dimensions	Customer Satisfaction (r)	Word of Mouth (r)	Recommen- dations to others (r)	Future Patronage (r)
Tangibles	0.54	0.53	0.55	0.43
Reliability	0.65	0.47	0.52	0.47
Responsiveness	0.58	0.54	0.55	0.51
Assurance	0.48	0.49	0.50	0.38
Empathy	0.43	0.47	0.53	0.44
Average Rating	0.65	0.58	0.62	0.53

r > 0.196 for significance at 5% level ;   r > 0.234 for significance at 1% level

All the five dimensions of SERVQUAL and its average rating were significantly correlated with customer satisfaction and the three variables of behavioural intentions. 'Reliability' and 'Average Rating' were strongly correlated with customer satisfaction. On the other hand, the correlation between 'Assurance' and 'Future Patronage' was relatively weak (0.38).

Multiple regression of SERVQUAL dimensions on Customer Satisfaction and Behavioural Intentions

When the ratings on the five dimensions of SERVQUAL were regressed on customer satisfaction and the three measures of behavioural intentions, the adjusted R^2 obtained were 0.44, 0.36, 0.30 and 0.35 respectively. The resultant output from the multiple regression is shown in in the Table below. The detailed analysis is shown in *Appendix 4.*

Table 12.10 : Multiple Regression – SERVQUAL

SERVQUAL	Customer Satisfaction		Word of Mouth		Recommenda- tion to others		Future Patronage	
	T value	Sig.	T value	Sig.	T value	Sig.	T value	Sig.
Tangibles	2.06	0.03**	15.05	<.001*	14.00	<.001*	8.57	<.001*
Reliability	13.34	<.001*	-2.06	0.04**	1.00	0.27	4.64	<.001*
Responsive-ness	10.84	<.001*	14.26	<.001*	11.97	<.001*	15.66	<.001*
Assurance	8.64	<.001*	4.22	<.001*	2.06	0.04**	-5.50	<.001*
Empathy	-0.16	0.91	2.49	0.01*	7.35	<.001*	4.14	<.001*
	F = 616.75 Sig F = .000		F = 445.49 Sig F = .000		F = 510.04 Sig F = .000		F = 336.47 Sig F = .000	
	* Significant at 1% level ** Significant at 5% level							

The resultant output from the multiple regression in Table 12.10 above yielded all significant dimensions except for the following : i)   Reliability on 'Recommendation to others'

ii)   Empathy on Customer Satisfaction

This result is apparently contrary to what was obtained from the correlations depicted in Table 4.8 on the previous page. The reason for this could be the problem of correlated independent variables, which means that when all other variables are accounted for, the contribution of say 'Empathy' or 'Reliability' beyond this is not significant, i.e. the contribution of 'Empathy' or 'Reliability' was captured through the other independent variables which they were related to.

Further research is necessary to understand the complicated causal relationships between the dependent and independent variables.

Relationship between Customised Scale, Customer Satisfaction and Behavioural Intentions.

Correlations

Pearson's Correlation was used to investigate the relationship of factors of the customised scale with customer satisfaction and behavioural intentions. This is shown in the Table below.

Table 12.11 : Correlation Coefficients (r) of Customised Scale with Customer Satisfaction and Behavioural Intentions

Factors of the Customised Scale	Customer Satisfaction (r)	Word of Mouth (r)	Recommen- dations to others (r)	Future Patronage (r)
Liner Service Personnel	0.68	0.57	0.56	0.49
On-board Services	0.41	0.35	0.54	0.54
Operational Features	0.40	0.41	0.40	0.27
Supplementary Services	0.16	0.11	0.22	0.25
Average Rating	0.56	0.48	0.57	0.54

r > 0.196 for significance at 5% level ; r > 0.234 for significance at 1% level

'Liner Service Personnel' and the Average Rating were strongly correlated with Customer Satisfaction and the three variables of Behavioural Intentions. There was no significant correlation (at 5% level) between 'Supplementary Services' and Customer Satisfaction / Word of Mouth. 'On-board Services' was strongly correlated with 'Recommendation to others' and 'Future Patronage'. Generally 'Operational Features' displayed a relatively weaker significant relationship with Customer Satisfaction and the three variables of Behavioural Intentions. Some of the items included in 'Operational Features' were comfortable ships, attractive ambience, photo gallery facilities, spacious rooms and efficient check-in/check-out facilities.

Multiple regression of the Customised Scale factors on Customer Satisfaction and Behavioural Intentions

When the ratings on the four factors of the Customised Scale were regressed on customer satisfaction and the three measures of behavioural intentions, the adjusted R^2 obtained were 0.56, 0.35, 0.39 and 0.34 respectively. The resultant output from the multiple regression is shown in the Table below. The detailed analysis is shown in *Appendix 4.*

Table 12.12 : Multiple Regression – Customised Scale

Customised Scale	Customer Satisfaction		Word of Mouth		Recommenda-tion to others		Future Patronage	
	T value	Sig.	T value	Sig.	T value	Sig.	T value	Sig.
Liner Service Personnel	39.41	<.001*	27.35	<.001*	18.48	<.001*	16.94	<.001*
On-board Services	4.30	<.001*	3.79	<.001*	21.41	<.001*	22.58	<.001*
Operational Features	0.69	0.48	8.11	<.001*	90.03	<.001*	-4.28	<.001*
Supplementary Services	-8.31	<.001*	-10.41	<.001*	37.61	<.001*	0.21	0.83
	F = 834.28 Sig F = .000		F = 529.09 Sig F = .000		F = 629.42 Sig F = .000		F = 505.65 Sig F = .000	
	* Significant at 1% level							

The resultant output from the multiple regression in Table 4.11 above yielded all significant factors except for the following : i) Operational Features on Customer Satisfaction

ii) Supplementary Services on Future Patronage

Hypotheses H_o2 and H_o4 were rejected. It is interesting to note that Operational Features (which constitutes 9 items) did not have a significant individual relationship with Customer Satisfaction. Also Supplementary Services (which constitutes 8 items) did not have a significant individual relationship with Future Patronage. However the problem of correlated independent variables as explained in 4.7.2 earlier should be considered. Further research is necessary to understand the complicated causal relationships between the dependent and independent variables.

12.12 Differences in behavioural intentions

Customer groups based on demographics and travel behaviour variables

Respondents were categorised into different groups based on demographics and their travel behaviour. These groups are listed in the Table below.

Table 12.13 : Customer Groups based on Demographics and Travel Behaviour

Demographics & Travel Behaviour	Group 1	Group 2	Group 3	Group 4
Gender	Male n = 108	Female n = 82		
Marital Status	Single n = 66	Married n = 110	Others n = 14	
Age	Below 25 years n = 34	25 to 45 years n = 112	Above 45 years n = 44	
Income	No income n = 47	Less than $ 5000 per month n = 91	Above $ 5000 per month n = 52	
Education	Secondary school n = 45	A-levels / Polytechnic n = 75	University and above n = 70	
Occupation	Not working n = 44	Clerical n = 19	Managerial n = 93	Own Business n = 34
Cruise experience	Experienced n = 76	Inexperienced n = 114		
Class of Travel	Stateroom n = 127	Stateroom with balcony n = 57	Suite n = 5	
Cabin Category	Twin n = 90	Triple n = 39	Quad n = 60	
Journey Accompaniment	Alone n = 2	With Family n = 109	In a Group n = 79	

102

Differences in Behavioural Intentions between groups

One-way ANOVA was used to determine if there were any significant differences in the mean scores of the three behavioural intention variables, between categories of respondents based on their demographic profile and travel behaviour. In cases where significant differences in more than two groups were identified, Post-Hoc tests were performed. The results of ANOVA and Post-Hoc tests are shown in the Tables below . The detailed analysis is shown in *Appendix 4.*

Table 12.14 : Tests of Mean Differences in scores of 'Word of Mouth'

Demographics & Travel Behaviour	Group 1		Group 2		Group 3		Group 4		ANOVA Sig *	Post-Hoc Test
	Mean	Std. Dev	Mean	Std. Dev	Mean	Std. Dev	Mean	Std. Dev		
Gender	5.97	0.92	5.90	0.91					No	
Marital Status	5.80	0.93	6.00	0.93					Yes *	
Age	5.66	1.02	5.97	0.86	6.09	0.92			Yes *	1 and 3**
Income	5.78	0.96	5.91	0.87	6.17	0.91			Yes *	1 and 3**
Education	5.86	0.99	5.88	0.84	6.06	0.91			Yes *	1 and 3**
Occupation	5.71	0.94	5.95	0.96	5.97	0.87	6.17	0.89	Yes *	1 and 4**
Cruise experience	5.97	0.94	6.02	0.88					No	
Class of Travel	5.76	1.01	5.98	0.94	6.25	0.50			No	
Cabin Category	6.14	0.88	5.84	0.78	5.88	0.99			No	
Journey Accomp.	6.04	0.91	5.89	0.88					No	

* Significant at 1 % level   ** groups listed were significantly different at 5% level

In the above Table significant differences were observed in the mean scores of the behavioural intention variable 'Word of Mouth' between respondents of different groups based on their marital status, age, income, education and occupation. The following groups of respondents gave the lowest scores when they were asked whether they would say positive things about Star Cruises to other people:

Those who were single, below 25 years old, who had no income (students, housewives,

103

retirees), those who had only secondary school education and those who were not working (students, housewives and retirees).

Table 12.15: Tests of Mean Differences in scores of 'Recommendation to others'

Demographics & Travel Behaviour	Group 1		Group 2		Group 3		Group 4		ANOVA Sig *	Post-Hoc Test
	Mean	Std. Dev	Mean	Std. Dev	Mean	Std. Dev	Mean	Std. Dev		
Gender	5.83	0.87	5.87	0.93					No	
Marital Status	5.79	0.77	5.90	0.97					Yes*	
Age	5.82	0.77	5.82	0.89	5.92	0.98			Yes*	1 & 3**
Income	5.74	1.02	5.89	0.77	5.85	0.96			Yes*	1 & 2**
Education	5.88	1.05	5.76	0.78	5.91	0.86			Yes*	2 & 3**
Occupation	5.66	1.00	5.88	0.78	5.82	0.79	6.12	0.97	Yes*	1 & 4**
Cruise experience	5.85	0.94	5.88	0.85					No	
Class of Travel	5.76	0.94	5.84	0.87	6.00	0.71			No	
Cabin Category	6.04	0.86	5.65	0.76	5.74	0.94			No	
Journey Accomp.	5.86	0.93	5.82	0.79					No	

* Significant at 1 % level   ** groups listed were significantly different at 5% level

In the above Table significant differences were observed in the mean scores of the behavioural intention variable 'Recommendation to others' between respondents of different groups based on their marital status, age, income, education and occupation. The following groups of respondents gave the lowest scores when they were asked whether they would recommend Star Cruises and also encourage their friends and relatives to travel on cruises operated by Star Cruises :

Those who were single, below 25 years old, who had no income (students, housewives, retirees), those who had A-Levels / Polytechnic education and those who were not working (students, housewives and retirees).

Table 12.16 : Tests of Mean Differences in scores of 'Future Patronage'

Demographics & Travel Behaviour	Group 1		Group 2		Group 3		Group 4		ANOVA Sig *	Post-Hoc Test
	Mean	Std. Dev	Mean	Std. Dev	Mean	Std. Dev	Mean	Std. Dev		
Gender	5.26	1.09	5.62	1.19					Yes *	
Marital Status	5.54	0.93	5.46	1.25					Yes *	
Age	5.60	0.83	5.45	1.21	5.23	1.21			Yes *	1 & 3 **
Income	5.31	1.09	5.62	1.11	5.17	1.22			Yes *	2 & 3 **
Education	5.66	1.11	5.39	1.09	5.28	1.21			Yes *	1 & 3 **
Occupation	5.28	1.11	5.64	0.91	5.35	1.14	5.64	1.29	Yes *	1 & 2 **
Cruise experience	5.24	1.26	5.59	1.06					No	
Class of Travel	5.51	1.21	5.19	1.17	4.50	0.58			No	
Cabin Category	5.57	1.15	5.38	1.09	5.30	1.22			No	
Journey Accomp.	5.34	1.23	5.34	1.23	5.54	1.03			No	

* Significant at 1 % level   ** groups listed were significantly different at 5% level

In the above Table significant differences were observed in the mean scores of the behavioural intention variable 'Future Patronage' between respondents of different groups based on their gender, marital status, age, income, education and occupation. The following groups of respondents gave the lowest scores when they were asked whether they would consider Star Cruises as their first choice to travel on a cruise :

Males, those who were married, above 45 years old, earning highest salaries, those who had university education and those who were not working (students, housewives and retirees).

CHAPTER 13: CONCLUSION, IMPLICATIONS & RECOMMENDATIONS

13.1 Conclusion

Companies must be customer oriented in an increasingly competitive environment (Kotler, 1997). After all, the underpinning of the marketing concept is that identification and satisfaction of customer needs leads to improved customer retention (Day, 1990). It is thus not surprising that companies associated with the hospitality industry spend substantial resources to measure and manage customer satisfaction. Overall customer satisfaction is extremely important as high customer satisfaction should indicate increased loyalty for current customers, reduced price elasticity, insulation from competitive efforts, lower costs of future transactions, reduced failure costs, lower costs of attracting new customers and an enhanced reputation for the firm (Fornell et al., 1996). This is especially true in the luxury cruise industry, where cruise operators focus on reusing the experienced passenger more often instead of reaching the first-time cruiser. This study was therefore conducted to present a comprehensive investigation of cruise travellers' overall customer satisfaction (CS), favourable behavioural intentions (BI) and the interrelationship between CS and BI. The major findings of this study can be summarised as :

Overall Customer Satisfaction :

Overall customer satisfaction was rated consistently high across all the categories of respondents. All the five dimensions of SERVQUAL and its average rating were significantly correlated with customer satisfaction. Multiple regression of SERVQUAL dimensions on customer satisfaction yielded all significant dimensions except for 'Empathy'. However, this result should be used with caution as it is difficult to interpret the actual effect of correlated independent variables (in this case Empathy) on dependent variables (in this case Customer Satisfaction).

When the customised scale was used it was found that 'Liner Service Personnel' and the average rating were strongly correlated with customer satisfaction. Multiple regression of the customised scale on customer satisfaction yielded all significant factors except for 'Operational Features'.

Behavioural Intentions :

Cruise travellers were asked questions about their likelihood of :

- saying positive things about the cruise to other people

106

- recommending the cruise to others
- future patronage (loyalty)

The mean scores of the 3 items were 5.94, 5.84 and 5.42 respectively (scores were taken on a scale of 1 to 7).

All the five dimensions of SERVQUAL and its average rating were significantly correlated with the three variables of behavioural intentions. Multiple regression of SERVQUAL dimensions with the three variables of behavioural intentions yielded all significant dimensions except for 'Reliability' on 'Recommendation to others'. However, this result should be used with caution as it is difficult to interpret the actual effect of correlated independent variables (in this case 'Reliability') on dependent variables (in this case 'Recommendation to others').

When the customised scale was used it was found that 'Liner Service Personnel' and the average rating were strongly correlated with the three variables of behavioural intentions. Also 'On-board Services' was strongly correlated with 'Recommendation to others' and 'Future Patronage'. Multiple regression of the customised scale on the three variables of behavioural intentions yielded all significant factors except for 'Supplementary Services' on 'Future Patronage'.

The post-purchase behavioural intentions of cruise travellers were analysed using their demographic profile and travel behaviour. A summary of significant behavioural intentions across the various segments is shown in Table 13.1 on the next page.

Table 13.1 : Summary of differences in Behavioural Intentions across different segments

Behavioural Intentions	Gender	Marital Status	Age	Personal Income	Level of Education	Occupation
Word-of-mouth		Singles lower than Married	Below 25 years lower than Above 45 years	No Income lower than those whose Income > $5000	Secondary school lower than University	Not working lower than Own Business
Recommenda-tion to Others		Singles lower than Married	Below 25 years lower than Above 45 years	No Income lower than those whose Income > $5000	A-Levels and Polytechnic lower than University	Now working lower than Own Business
Future Patronage	Males lower than Females	Married lower than Singles	Above 45 years lower than below 25 years	Income >$5000 lower than Income < $5000	University lower than Secondary School	Not Working lower than Clerical Staff and Own Business

There were no significant differences in the mean scores of the three behavioural intentions across segments of respondents based on their travel behaviour, namely, previous cruise experience, class of travel, cabin category and journey accompaniment.

From the above Table it can be seen that significantly lower ratings were given for Word-of-mouth related behavioural intentions by singles, below 25 years old, those who had only secondary school education, housewives, students and retirees.

For the second variable of behavioural intentions, i.e. 'Recommendation to others' respondents who belonged to one of the following groups gave significantly low ratings : singles, below 25 years old, students, housewives and retirees and those who had A-levels or Polytechnic education.

For the last variable of behavioural intentions, i.e. 'Future Patronage' significantly lower ratings were given by respondents who were males, married, above 45 years old, earning highest salaries, those who had university education and students, housewives and retirees. Star Cruises may wish to rectify this situation especially as regards travellers who are married, above 45 years old and those who are earning high salaries. They should also take advantage of the knowledge about the categories of respondents which have given high ratings for 'Future Patronage'.

Relationship between CS and BI

This study revealed that overall satisfaction had a relatively strong relationship with all the three variables of BI. This finding is in line with the findings of similar studies undertaken in the area of post-purchase behavioural intentions. Also, the relationship between overall satisfaction was higher with 'Word of mouth' and 'Recommendation' than with 'Future Patronage'. Presumably this was because some travellers even though they are satisfied and happy to tell others, might consider a cruise to be a one-off experience, something they are not likely to want to do again.

Recent research offers some evidence that CS perceptions positively affect BI. However, most of the research operationalises BI in a unidimensional way rather than delineate specific types of behaviour. For example, Anderson and Sullivan (1993) in analysing data from a study of customer satisfaction among Swedish consumers, find that stated repurchase intention is strongly related to stated satisfaction across product categories. A study conducted by Woodside et al (1989) uncovers a significant association between overall patient satisfaction and intent to choose the hospital again.

13.2 Implications for Cruise Operators

This study, which has contributed to the services marketing and customer satisfaction literature, has revealed that the key to customer creation and retention appears to be the fostering of favourable behavioural intentions among cruise travellers.

By focusing on the cumulative perspective of the construct, the dominant "disconfirmation of expectation" paradigm was critiqued and not adopted in this study.

The classification of customer satisfaction into its components will enrich the conceptual implication of the construct, enhance its predicting power in explaining other variables like behavioural intentions and increase diagnostic information for satisfaction management.

Additionally, despite the widely used single item measure of the construct, this study has established excellent measurement scales for the components of customer satisfaction. Although these measurements were focused on the leisure cruise industry, they can be adjusted to accommodate a broad range of other service sectors.

The results of this study manifested many managerial implications pertaining to satisfaction measurement and management, strategic planning and internal marketing.

Such measurements are needed to track trends, to diagnose problems and to link to other customer-focused strategies. Because every service encounter is potentially critical to customer retention, many firms aim for "zero defects" or 100 percent satisfaction. To achieve this requires clear documentation of all the points of contact between the organisation and its customers.

The measurement scales for overall satisfaction developed in this study can help cruise operators to establish satisfaction measurement systems to monitor their service performance and customer satisfaction. A marketing system based on the scales is expected to provide more accurate, complete and useful diagnostic information that can facilitate the improvement of cruise operation and services. A battery of behavioural intentions can be incorporated into the system to capture the satisfaction effects and to diagnose the sources of unfavourable behavioural intentions.

This study offers empirical examination for the intuitive notion that enhancing customer satisfaction can increase favourable behavioural intentions and decrease unfavourable intentions. This can establish the basis for companies' strategic planning to invest in improving customer satisfaction. Companies that are devoted to improving customer satisfaction can gain more confidence from this study.

It has been observed that the relationships between customer satisfaction and behavioural intentions had different strengths across different segments of cruise travellers. If a cruise operator can determine the customer-related variables that moderate the satisfaction-intention link, it would be a profitable deal to focus the satisfaction improvement efforts on the group of travellers who score favourable on those variables, and to adjust the service operations to accommodate the needs of those travellers.

Lastly, retention strategies will have little long-term success unless there is a solid base of service quality and customer satisfaction to build on.

13.3 Limitations and Suggestions for Future Research

Although the overall results of this study are quite encouraging, their implications may be limited by several considerations.

The results cannot be generalised across the entire cruise and hospitality industries. This study collected data from travellers on a modern cruise liner. Hence the sample may not represent the entirety of cruise travellers. There could be substantial differences in the overall customer satisfaction and behavioural intention ratings of travellers sailing on older cruise liners. Similar studies should be replicated by including more diversified subjects, which may then increase the chances of generalising the results.

The behavioural-intention battery used in this study needs further development. In particular, more items are needed to strengthen the reliability of its components. Favourable intentions like 'spend more with company' and 'pay price premium' and also several types of unfavourable intentions should be investigated.

The findings of this survey should be used together with the findings of in-depth interviews conducted on board the liner with travellers who are randomly selected.

A more detailed study with respect to the behavioural intentions of passengers on board cruise liners should be made. This should include :

- Differences in behavioural intentions among respondents with service quality perceptions that fall above, within or below their zone of tolerance.

- Impact of service problems and service recovery on behavioural intentions.

Structural equation modeling using Lisrel VIII can be used to test the path coefficients of customer satisfaction and various aspects of behavioural intentions.

Finally, further research on the association between behavioural intentions and remaining with or defecting from the cruise company merits study. Zahorik and Rust (1993) suggest ways to investigate this link, including panel data, longitudinal analysis with customers and cross-sectional surveys asking customers about previous and current providers.

SERVICES OFFERED BY STAR CRUISES

This research survey seeks to examine the level of Service Quality offered by Star Cruises. Please answer the following questions based on your knowledge and experience. There are no right or wrong answers. Your responses will be kept **strictly confidential** and only aggregated results (not individual responses) will be mentioned in the research outputs.

SECTION A

Please tick against the appropriate answer

1. Have you ever been on a cruise with Star Cruises before this one ?

    ❏ Yes   ❏ No

    If your answer to the above question is yes, please also answer Question 2. If not please proceed to Question 3.

2. Which of the following ships did you take your cruise on before this one :

    ➤   Superstar Leo -   No. of cruises   :   1   2   3   4
    ➤   Star Aquarius -   No. of cruises   :   1   2   3   4
    ➤   Superstar Gemini -   No. of cruises   :   1   2   3   4

3. Have you ever been on a cruise with any other cruise companies before ?

    ❏ Yes   ❏ No

4. In which class are you travelling on this cruise ?

    ❏ Inside Stateroom   ❏ Ocean view   ❏ Ocean view Stateroom
                              Stateroom with window   with Balcony

    ❏ Zodiac Suite   ❏ Executive Suite
      /Galazy Suite

5. In which category of cabin are you travelling on this cruise ?

    ❏ Twin   ❏ Triple   ❏ Quad

6. How are you travelling on this cruise :

    ❏ Alone   ❏ With spouse only   ❏ With spouse and children

    ❏ With partner ❏ With friends/   ❏ With relatives
                      colleagues in a
                      group

SECTION B

In the 1st column we are interested to find out what you expect from a high performing cruise liner. Based on your experience, please think about any cruise liner that would deliver excellent quality of service. Please show the extent to which you think such a cruise liner would possess the feature described below. If you feel that a feature is *not at all essential* for excellent cruise liners such as the one you have in mind, circle the number **1**. If you feel that a feature is *absolutely essential* for excellent cruise liners, circle number **7**. If your **expectations** are less strong, circle one of the numbers in the middle. There are no right or wrong answers.

In the 2nd column we are interested to find out your evaluation of services performed by **Star Cruises**. Please indicate the extent to which you feel that **Star Cruises** have the features stated below. Once again, circling **1** means that you strongly disagree that Star Cruises have that feature, and circling **7** means that you strongly agree. You may circle any of the numbers in the middle that show how strong your feelings are. There are no right or wrong answers – all we are interested in is a number that best shows your **perceptions** about services performed by **Star Cruises**.

Features of Cruise Liners	A High Performing Cruise Line will		Star Cruises	
	Strongly Disagree	**Strongly Agree**	**Strongly Disagree**	**Strongly Agree**
1. Have a modern fleet of ships	1 2 3 4 5 6 7		1 2 3 4 5 6 7	
2. Have attractive ambience and décor on their ships	1 2 3 4 5 6 7		1 2 3 4 5 6 7	
3. Have employees with professional appearance...	1 2 3 4 5 6 7		1 2 3 4 5 6 7	
4. Charge low fares for the cruises	1 2 3 4 5 6 7		1 2 3 4 5 6 7	
5. Have employees who meet passengers' requests in a reasonable time	1 2 3 4 5 6 7		1 2 3 4 5 6 7	
6. Handle complaints from passengers promptly	1 2 3 4 5 6 7		1 2 3 4 5 6 7	
7. Have employees who rarely make mistakes.....	1 2 3 4 5 6 7		1 2 3 4 5 6 7	
8. Meet needs of passengers correctly upon first request	1 2 3 4 5 6 7		1 2 3 4 5 6 7	
9. Carry out passengers' requests or instructions without error	1 2 3 4 5 6 7		1 2 3 4 5 6 7	
10.Have employees who are concerned, responsive and attentive to passengers' needs.............	1 2 3 4 5 6 7		1 2 3 4 5 6 7	

Features of Cruise Liners	A High Performing Cruise Line will		Star Cruises	
	Strongly Disagree	Strongly Agree	Strongly Disagree	Strongly Agree
11. Have employees who provide prompt services...	1 2 3 4 5 6 7		1 2 3 4 5 6 7	
12. Have employees who are always willing to help..	1 2 3 4 5 6 7		1 2 3 4 5 6 7	
13. Have employees who always find time to meet passengers' requests	1 2 3 4 5 6 7		1 2 3 4 5 6 7	
14. Have employees who instill confidence	1 2 3 4 5 6 7		1 2 3 4 5 6 7	
15. Make passengers feel safe	1 2 3 4 5 6 7		1 2 3 4 5 6 7	
16. Have courteous and polite employees	1 2 3 4 5 6 7		1 2 3 4 5 6 7	
17. Have employees who are competent in performing their duties	1 2 3 4 5 6 7		1 2 3 4 5 6 7	
18. Have employees who pay individualised attention to passengers.........................	1 2 3 4 5 6 7		1 2 3 4 5 6 7	
19. Have convenient arrival/departure times....	1 2 3 4 5 6 7		1 2 3 4 5 6 7	
20. Have employees who understand the needs of different nationalities	1 2 3 4 5 6 7		1 2 3 4 5 6 7	
21. Have employees who are sympathetic and reassuring when passengers encounter problems	1 2 3 4 5 6 7		1 2 3 4 5 6 7	
22. Meet the needs of special passengers (e.g. elderly, handicapped, infants, etc)	1 2 3 4 5 6 7		1 2 3 4 5 6 7	
23. Have spacious rooms to sleep and relax comfortably	1 2 3 4 5 6 7		1 2 3 4 5 6 7	
24. Serve delicious and tasty food	1 2 3 4 5 6 7		1 2 3 4 5 6 7	
25. Have ships which are comfortable to sail on....	1 2 3 4 5 6 7		1 2 3 4 5 6 7	
26. Have good Casino and Jackpot facilities.......	1 2 3 4 5 6 7		1 2 3 4 5 6 7	
27. Have wide passageways for easy movement ...	1 2 3 4 5 6 7		1 2 3 4 5 6 7	
28. Have good signs, posters and instructions for easy movement on their ships..................	1 2 3 4 5 6 7		1 2 3 4 5 6 7	

Features of Cruise Liners	A High Performing Cruise Line will		Star Cruises	
	Strongly Disagree	Strongly Agree	Strongly Disagree	Strongly Agree
29. Visit many ports of destinations................	1 2 3 4 5 6 7		1 2 3 4 5 6 7	
30. Have clean and well maintained ships.......	1 2 3 4 5 6 7		1 2 3 4 5 6 7	
31. Serve food that is fresh	1 2 3 4 5 6 7		1 2 3 4 5 6 7	
32. Have good security arrangements	1 2 3 4 5 6 7		1 2 3 4 5 6 7	
33. Have good arrangements for shore excursions...	1 2 3 4 5 6 7		1 2 3 4 5 6 7	
34. Provide food that caters to needs of different passengers (e.g. vegetarian food, halal food, baby food, low-fat/calories, diabetic diet etc)..	1 2 3 4 5 6 7		1 2 3 4 5 6 7	
35. Have fast and efficient check-in and check-out facilities......................................	1 2 3 4 5 6 7		1 2 3 4 5 6 7	
36. Provide a variety of beverages on the cruise....	1 2 3 4 5 6 7		1 2 3 4 5 6 7	
37. Have good communication (telephone, fax, Internet) facilities on board ships.............	1 2 3 4 5 6 7		1 2 3 4 5 6 7	
38. Have good gift and duty free shops	1 2 3 4 5 6 7		1 2 3 4 5 6 7	
39. Have employees who are energetic looking....	1 2 3 4 5 6 7		1 2 3 4 5 6 7	
40. Provide a variety of main courses of food that passengers can choose from..................	1 2 3 4 5 6 7		1 2 3 4 5 6 7	
41. Show care and concern for passengers when the cruises do not depart or arrive on time.....	1 2 3 4 5 6 7		1 2 3 4 5 6 7	
42. Conduct proper Safety Drills to demonstrate procedures in cases of emergencies............	1 2 3 4 5 6 7		1 2 3 4 5 6 7	
43. Have a good selection of magazines, newsstudys and books on board..............	1 2 3 4 5 6 7		1 2 3 4 5 6 7	
44. Provide amenities (e.g. extra pillows, blankets, towels, etc) to passengers.....................	1 2 3 4 5 6 7		1 2 3 4 5 6 7	
45. Inform travellers of any delays to the cruise departures well in advance...................	1 2 3 4 5 6 7		1 2 3 4 5 6 7	

Features of Cruise Liners	A High Performing Cruise Line will ...		Star Cruises	
	Strongly Disagree	Strongly Agree	Strongly Disagree	Strongly Agree
46. Have prompt meal and beverage services	1 2 3 4 5 6 7		1 2 3 4 5 6 7	
47. Have employees who are dependable in their service delivery.............................	1 2 3 4 5 6 7		1 2 3 4 5 6 7	
48. Are punctual in departure and arrival time...	1 2 3 4 5 6 7		1 2 3 4 5 6 7	
49. Treat passengers fairly, without any bias.......	1 2 3 4 5 6 7		1 2 3 4 5 6 7	
50. Have reliable baggage handling facilities.....	1 2 3 4 5 6 7		1 2 3 4 5 6 7	
51. Provide accurate voyage information on board ships......................................	1 2 3 4 5 6 7		1 2 3 4 5 6 7	
52. Have good safety records and ISM certification	1 2 3 4 5 6 7		1 2 3 4 5 6 7	
53. Serve adequate snacks in between meals	1 2 3 4 5 6 7		1 2 3 4 5 6 7	
54. Have some staff on board ship who can speak other major languages besides English	1 2 3 4 5 6 7		1 2 3 4 5 6 7	
55. Handle reservation services efficiently.......	1 2 3 4 5 6 7		1 2 3 4 5 6 7	
56. Have convenient ticket reservation system.....	1 2 3 4 5 6 7		1 2 3 4 5 6 7	
57. Impose few restrictions when travellers' cruise plans are changed (e.g. deposit will not be forfeited, no fines imposed etc)......	1 2 3 4 5 6 7		1 2 3 4 5 6 7	
58. Provide courteous telephone service	1 2 3 4 5 6 7		1 2 3 4 5 6 7	
59. Make timely and clear announcements.......	1 2 3 4 5 6 7		1 2 3 4 5 6 7	
60. Have proper lost baggage procedures.........	1 2 3 4 5 6 7		1 2 3 4 5 6 7	
61. Are flexible and bend rules for its passengers...	1 2 3 4 5 6 7		1 2 3 4 5 6 7	
62. Receive strong support from its travel agents...	1 2 3 4 5 6 7		1 2 3 4 5 6 7	
63. Offer frequent traveller programmes............	1 2 3 4 5 6 7		1 2 3 4 5 6 7	
64. Have hassle-free pre-boarding security screenings...	1 2 3 4 5 6 7		1 2 3 4 5 6 7	

Features of Cruise Liners	A High Performing Cruise Line will ...		Star Cruises	
	Strongly Disagree	Strongly Agree	Strongly Disagree	Strongly Agree
65. Have good video arcade facilities.............	1 2 3 4 5 6 7		1 2 3 4 5 6 7	
66. Have good sports and fitness facilities........	1 2 3 4 5 6 7		1 2 3 4 5 6 7	
67. Have good medical and health services.......	1 2 3 4 5 6 7		1 2 3 4 5 6 7	
68. Have good photo gallery facilities.............	1 2 3 4 5 6 7		1 2 3 4 5 6 7	
69. Have good arrangements for viewing the ship's bridge and other places of interest on the ship...	1 2 3 4 5 6 7		1 2 3 4 5 6 7	
70. Have good passenger accounting and billing facilities on board ships........................	1 2 3 4 5 6 7		1 2 3 4 5 6 7	
71. Have good cabin maintenance and cleaning facilities	1 2 3 4 5 6 7		1 2 3 4 5 6 7	
72. Have good entertainment facilities for children..	1 2 3 4 5 6 7		1 2 3 4 5 6 7	
73. Have good shows and entertainment for adults...	1 2 3 4 5 6 7		1 2 3 4 5 6 7	
74. Have ships which behave well whilst sailing, thus reducing chances of sea-sickness.......	1 2 3 4 5 6 7		1 2 3 4 5 6 7	
75. Have good child care facilities on board....	1 2 3 4 5 6 7		1 2 3 4 5 6 7	

Considering all the aspects, how would you rate the overall Service Quality of this Cruise. (*Please circle the appropriate number*)

Very Poor   *Excellent*
1   2   3   4   5   6   7

SECTION C

Listed below are 5 features pertaining to Cruise Lines and the services they offer. We would like to know how important each of these features is to you when you evaluate a particular Cruise Line. Please *allocate a total of 100 points among the five features according to how important each feature is to you* – the more important a feature is to you, the more points you should allocate to it. Please ensure that the points you allocate to the five features add up to 100.

a. The appearance of the Cruise Line's physical facilities, equipment, personnel and communication materials.

_____ points

b. The ability of the Cruise Line to perform the promised service dependably and accurately.

_____ points

c. The willingness of the Cruise Line to help passengers and to provide prompt service.

_____ points

d. The knowledge and courtesy of the Cruise Line's employees and their ability to convey trust and confidence.

_____ points

e. The caring, personalised attention which the Cruise Line provides to its passengers.

_____ points

TOTAL points allocated   **100 points**

SECTION D

The following questions are for classification purposes only and will be kept strictly confidential. *(Please tick against the appropriate box)*

1. What is your gender ?

   ❑ Male ❑ Female

2. What is your nationality ?

   ❑ Singaporean ❑ Others   Please specify : _____

3. If you are a Singaporean, what is your race ?

   ❑ Chinese ❑ Malay ❑ Indian ❑ Others

4. What is your marital status ?

   ❑ Single ❑ Married ❑ Divorced ❑ Widowed

5. To which of the following age group do you belong ?

   ❑ Below 25 ❑ 25 to 34 ❑ 35 to 44 ❑ 45 to 55 ❑ 55 and above

6. Based on your gross personal income (before CPF contributions and taxes), which category do you belong to ?

   ❑ Not working (housewife/student/NS/retiree)   ❑ Less than $ 2000 per month   ❑ $ 2000 to $ 3500 per month

   ❑ $ 3501 to $ 5000 per month   ❑ $ 5001 to $ 6500 per month   ❑ Above $ 6500 per month

7. What is your educational level ?

   ❑ Secondary school   ❑ A-Levels   ❑ Polytechnic Diploma   ❑ University Degree   ❑ Post graduate Degree

8. What is your occupation ?

   ❑ Not working (Home-maker/Student/NS)   ❑ Clerical/Production/Sales   ❑ Supervisory

   ❑ Junior Executive   ❑ Managerial/Profess-ional   ❑ Own Business/Self Employed

SECTION E

In this Section we would like to assess your feelings towards **Star Cruises** <u>after</u> you have been on a cruise with them. For each of the following statements please indicate your position by circling one of the numbers which is closest to your feelings.

	Not at all Likely						**Extremely likely**
1. Say positive things about Star Cruises to other people.	1	2	3	4	5	6	7
2. Recommend Star Cruises to someone who seeks your advice.	1	2	3	4	5	6	7
3. Encourage friends and relatives to travel on cruises operated by Star Cruises.	1	2	3	4	5	6	7
4. Consider Star Cruises as your first choice to travel on a cruise.	1	2	3	4	5	6	7

SECTION F

Based on your overall experience on this cruise, how **satisfied** are you with the Total Service Quality offered by Star Cruises. (*Please circle the appropriate number*)

Not At all Satisfied					*Very High Satisfaction*	
1	2	3	4	5	6	7

Thank you for taking the time to complete this survey.

Please be assured that your responses will be kept strictly confidential.

Appendix 2 – Item-by-Item Tests of Mean Differences

Item-by-Item Tests of Mean Differences (for Factor 3) by **Previous Cruise Experience**

Type of Traveller	30. Have clean and well maintained ships			25. Have ships which are comfortable to sail on			1. Have a modern fleet of ships			71. Have good cabin maintenance and cleaning facilities		
	Mean	Std. Dev	Sig. (p)	Mean	Std. Dev	Sig. (p)	Mean	Std. Dev	Sig. (p)	Mean	Std. Dev	Sig. (p)
Experienced	6.15	1.00		5.92	1.26		6.02	0.99		5.89	1.06	
			0.27			0.99			0.73			0.35
In-experienced	6.40	0.58		5.92	1.15		6.06	1.05		6.12	0.72	

Type Of Traveller	2. Have attractive ambience and décor on their ships			74. Have ships which behave well at sea			23. Have spacious rooms to sleep and relax comfortably			68. Have good photo gallery facilities			35. Have fast check-in and check-out facilities		
	Mean	Std. Dev	Sig. (p)	Mean	Std. Dev	Sig. (p)	Mean	Std. Dev	Sig. (p)	Mean	Std. Dev	Sig. (p)	Mean	Std. Dev	Sig. (p)
Experienced	6.15	0.82		5.92	1.21		5.32	1.17		5.07	1.26	*	5.14	1.33	*
			0.70			0.69			0.91			0.05			0.05
In-experienced	6.24	0.83		6.04	1.09		5.36	1.28		5.56	1.00		5.48	1.08	

* Significant at 5% level

Item-by-Item Tests of Mean Differences (for Factor 1) by **Cabin Category**

Cabin Category	8. Meet needs of passengers correctly upon first request			11. Have employees who provide prompt services			9. Carry out passengers' requests or instructions without error			17. Have employees who are competent in performing their duties		
	Mean	Std. Dev	Sig. (p)	Mean	Std. Dev	Sig. (p)	Mean	Std. Dev	Sig. (p)	Mean	Std. Dev	Sig. (p)
Twin	5.48	0.91	*	5.74	0.82		5.52	0.87		5.83	1.06	*
Quad	5.07	0.97	0.02	5.44	0.93	0.06	5.15	0.86	0.06	5.41	0.99	0.02

* Significant at 5 % level

Cabin Category	6. Handle complaints from passengers promptly			16. Have courteous and polite employees			3. Have employees with professional appearance			21. Have employees who are sympathetic and reassuring when passengers encounter problems		
	Mean	Std. Dev	Sig. (p)	Mean	Std. Dev	Sig. (p)	Mean	Std. Dev	Sig. (p)	Mean	Std. Dev	Sig. (p)
Twin	5.71	0.91	*	6.18	1.13	*	5.85	0.93		5.35	1.03	
Quad	5.12	1.15	0.00	5.68	1.14	0.03	5.57	0.94	0.07	5.13	1.14	0.11

* significant at 5% level

Item-by-Item Tests of Mean Differences (for Factor 1) by **Cabin Category**

Cabin Category	13. Have employees who always find time to meet passengers' requests			18. Have employees who pay individualised attention to passengers			12. Have employees who are always willing to help			7. Have employees who rarely make mistakes			5. Have employees who meet passengers' requests in a reasonable time		
	Mean	Std. Dev	Sig. (p)	Mean	Std. Dev	Sig. (p)	Mean	Std. Dev	Sig. (p)	Mean	Std. Dev	Sig. (p)	Mean	Std. Dev	Sig. (p)
Twin	5.61	0.83		5.04	1.04		5.83	0.84		5.03	0.97		5.79	0.85	*
Quad	5.29	0.87	0.12	4.82	0.95	0.07	5.49	0.84	0.09	4.67	1.13	0.06	5.28	1.02	0.03

* Significant at 5% level

Item-by-Item Tests of Mean Differences (for Factor 3) by **Cabin Category**

Cabin Category	30. Have clean and well maintained ships			25. Have ships which are comfortable to sail on			1. Have a modern fleet of ships			71. Have good cabin maintenance and cleaning facilities		
	Mean	Std. Dev	Sig. (p)	Mean	Std. Dev	Sig. (p)	Mean	Std. Dev	Sig. (p)	Mean	Std. Dev	Sig. (p)
Twin	6.64	0.63	*	6.42	0.86	*	6.34	0.81	*	6.45	0.67	*
Quad	6.28	0.80	0.02	6.04	1.09	0.01	5.93	0.86	0.01	6.03	0.89	0.01

Item-by-Item Tests of Mean Differences (for Factor 3) by **Cabin Category**

Cabin Category	2. Have attractive ambience and décor on their ships			74. Have ships which behave well at sea			23. Have spacious rooms to sleep and relax comfortably			68. Have good photo gallery facilities			35. Have fast check-in and check-out facilities		
	Mean	Std. Dev	Sig. (p)	Mean	Std. Dev	Sig. (p)	Mean	Std. Dev	Sig. (p)	Mean	Std. Dev	Sig. (p)	Mean	Std. Dev	Sig. (p)
Quad	6.40	0.71		6.34	1.07		5.77	0.97		5.62	1.14		5.60	1.00	
			0.54			* 0.01			* 0.00			0.23			* 0.03
Twin	6.31	0.69		5.85	1.18		5.23	1.13		5.31	1.05		5.21	1.33	

* Significant at 5% level

Item-by-Item Tests of Mean Differences (for Factor 4) by **Cabin Category**

Cabin Category	56. Have convenient ticket reservation system			62. Receive strong support from its travel agents			64. Have hassle-free pre-boarding security screenings			55. Handle reservation services efficiently		
	Mean	Std. Dev	Sig. (p)	Mean	Std. Dev	Sig. (p)	Mean	Std. Dev	Sig. (p)	Mean	Std. Dev	Sig. (p)
Twin	5.74	1.00		5.85	1.07		5.85	0.91		5.76	1.04	
			* 0.02			* 0.01			* 0.00			* 0.01
Quad	5.28	1.15		5.44	1.22		5.21	0.94		5.17	1.07	

* Significant at 5 % level

Item-by-Item Tests of Mean Differences (for Factor 4) by **Cabin Category**

Cabin Category	45. Inform travellers of any delays to the cruise departures well in advance			60. Have proper lost baggage procedures			63. Offer frequent traveller programmes			48. Are punctual in departure and arrival times		
	Mean	Std. Dev	Sig. (p)	Mean	Std. Dev	Sig. (p)	Mean	Std. Dev	Sig. (p)	Mean	Std. Dev	Sig. (p)
Twin	5.96	0.89		5.50	0.90		3.52	1.97		6.00	0.85	
Quad	5.78	0.85	0.15	5.35	0.99	0.32	3.42	1.45	0.48	5.93	1.03	0.65

*   significant at 5% level

Item-by-Item Tests of Mean Differences (for Factor 2) by **Travel Accompaniment**

Travel Accompani-ment	34.Provide food that caters to needs of different passengerss			31. Serve food that is fresh			36. Provide a variety of beverages			40. Provide a variety of main courses			69. Have good arrangements for viewing the ship's bridge		
	Mean	Std. Dev	Sig. (p)	Mean	Std. Dev	Sig. (p)	Mean	Std. Dev	Sig. (p)	Mean	Std. Dev	Sig. (p)	Mean	Std. Dev	Sig. (p)
With Family	4.67	1.38		5.08	1.07		4.48	1.51		4.64	1.20		4.46	1.42	
In a Group	4.66	1.07	0.93	5.23	1.18	0.35	4.87	1.18	* 0.03	4.91	1.02	0.16	5.04	1.39	* 0.01

*   Significant at 5% level

Item-by-Item Tests of Mean Differences (for Factor 2) by **Travel Accompaniment**

Travel Accompa-niment	24.Serves delicious and tasty food			73. Have good shows and entertainment for adults			26. Have good casino and jackpot facilities			53. Serve adequate snacks in between meals			33. Have good arrangements for shore excursions		
	Mean	Std. Dev	Sig. (p)	Mean	Std. Dev	Sig. (p)	Mean	Std. Dev	Sig. (p)	Mean	Std. Dev	Sig. (p)	Mean	Std. Dev	Sig. (p)
With Family	4.64	1.33		5.02	1.10		5.50	1.01		5.16	1.19	*	5.06	1.21	
In a Group	4.67	1.39	0.92	5.07	1.14	0.93	5.35	1.10	0.23	5.51	1.00	0.05	5.11	1.10	0.78

* Significant at 5% level

Item-by-Item Tests of Mean Differences (for Factor 3) by **Travel Accompaniment**

Travel Accompani-ment	30. Have clean and well maintained ships			25. Have ships which are comfortable to sail on			1. Have a modern fleet of ships			71. Have good cabin maintenance and cleaning facilities		
	Mean	Std. Dev	Sig. (p)	Mean	Std. Dev	Sig. (p)	Mean	Std. Dev	Sig. (p)	Mean	Std. Dev	Sig. (p)
With Family	6.60	0.68	*	6.35	0.96		6.31	0.85		6.39	0.75	
In a Group	6.35	0.69	0.04	6.05	1.09	0.15	6.04	0.95	0.08	5.98	0.85	0.06

* Significant at 5% level

Item-by-Item Tests of Mean Differences (for Factor 3) by **Travel Accompaniment**

Travel Accompaniment	2. Have attractive ambience and décor on their ships			74. Have ships which behave well at sea			23. Have spacious rooms to sleep and relax comfortably			68.Have good photo gallery facilities			35. Have fast check-in and check-out facilities		
	Mean	Std. Dev	Sig. (p)	Mean	Std. Dev	Sig. (p)	Mean	Std. Dev	Sig. (p)	Mean	Std. Dev	Sig. (p)	Mean	Std. Dev	Sig. (p)
With Family	6.41	0.79		6.50	0.79		5.60	1.19		5.46	1.14		5.33	1.38	
			0.35			* 0.00			* 0.00			0.61			0.48
In a Group	6.21	0.76		5.77	1.29		5.24	1.19		5.41	1.08		5.46	0.92	

* Significant at 5% level

Item-by-Item Tests of Mean Differences (for Factor 3) by **Marital Status**

Marital Status	30. Have clean and well maintained ships			25. Have ships which are comfortable to sail on			1. Have a modern fleet of ships			71. Have good cabin maintenance and cleaning facilities		
	Mean	Std. Dev	Sig. (p)	Mean	Std. Dev	Sig. (p)	Mean	Std. Dev	Sig. (p)	Mean	Std. Dev	Sig. (p)
Single	6.32	0.69		5.96	0.96		6.05	0.97		5.89	0.81	
			0.06			* 0.03			0.19			* 0.00
Married	6.55	0.71		6.32	0.99		6.24	0.88		6.41	0.79	

* Significant at 5% level

Item-by-Item Tests of Mean Differences (for Factor 3) by **Marital Status**

Marital Status	2. Have attractive ambience and décor on their ships			74. Have ships which behave well at sea			23. Have spacious rooms to sleep and relax comfortably			68.Have good photo gallery facilities			35. Have fast check-in and check-out facilities		
	Mean	Std. Dev	Sig. (p)	Mean	Std. Dev	Sig. (p)	Mean	Std. Dev	Sig. (p)	Mean	Std. Dev	Sig. (p)	Mean	Std. Dev	Sig. (p)
Single	6.15	0.75		5.85	1.26		5.11	1.17		5.45	1.14		5.50	1.81	
			0.34			* 0.00			* 0.03			0.87			0.15
Married	6.39	0.81		6.33	0.97		5.54	1.18		5.42	1.08		5.35	1.45	

* Significant at 5% level

Item-by-Item Tests of Mean Differences (for Factor 3) by **Age**

Age Group	30. Have clean and well maintained ships			25. Have ships which are comfortable to sail on			1. Have a modern fleet of ships			71. Have good cabin maintenance and cleaning facilities		
	Mean	Std. Dev	Sig. (p)	Mean	Std. Dev	Sig. (p)	Mean	Std. Dev	Sig. (p)	Mean	Std. Dev	Sig. (p)
Below 25 years	6.20	0.75		5.58	1.24		5.99	1.07		5.82	0.77	
			0.17			* 0.00			0.10			* 0.00
Above 45 years	6.50	0.67		6.39	0.80		6.31	0.81		6.39	0.76	

* Significant at 5% level

Item-by-Item Tests of Mean Differences (for Factor 3) by **Age**

Age	2. Have attractive ambience and décor on their ships			74. Have ships which behave well at sea			23. Have spacious rooms to sleep and relax comfortably			68.Have good photo gallery facilities			35. Have fast check-in and check-out facilities		
Group	Mean	Std. Dev	Sig. (p)	Mean	Std. Dev	Sig. (p)	Mean	Std. Dev	Sig. (p)	Mean	Std. Dev	Sig. (p)	Mean	Std. Dev	Sig. (p)
Below 25 years	6.16	0.82		5.56	1.46		5.00	1.12	*	5.54	1.00		5.49	0.87	
Above 45 years	6.30	0.88	0.56	6.17	1.06	0.12	5.84	1.12	0.00	5.44	1.12	0.90	5.45	1.15	0.93

* Significant at 5% level

Item-by-Item Tests of Mean Differences (for Factor 3) by **Personal Income**

Personal Income	30. Have clean and well maintained ships			25. Have ships which are comfortable to sail on			1. Have a modern fleet of ships			71. Have good cabin maintenance and cleaning facilities		
	Mean	Std. Dev	Sig. (p)	Mean	Std. Dev	Sig. (p)	Mean	Std. Dev	Sig. (p)	Mean	Std. Dev	Sig. (p)
No Income	6.19	0.85		5.74	1.24		5.88	1.11		6.01	0.85	
Less than $ 5000 p.m.	6.55	0.62	* 0.01	6.35	0.80	* 0.00	6.34	0.72	* 0.03	6.31	0.79	0.11

Item-by-Item Tests of Mean Differences (for Factor 3) by **Personal Income**

Personal Income	2. Have attractive ambience and décor on their ships			74. Have ships which behave well at sea			23. Have spacious rooms to sleep and relax comfortably			68.Have good photo gallery facilities			35. Have fast check-in and check-out facilities		
	Mean	Std. Dev	Sig. (p)	Mean	Std. Dev	Sig. (p)	Mean	Std. Dev	Sig. (p)	Mean	Std. Dev	Sig. (p)	Mean	Std. Dev	Sig. (p)
No Income	6.24	0.83		5.59	1.46		5.16	1.19		5.36	1.19		5.09	1.30	
			0.35			* 0.00			0.08			0.48			* 0.00
Less than $ 5000 p.m.	6.38	0.70		6.43	0.81		5.57	1.05		5.51	1.20		5.71	1.03	

*   Significant at 5% level

Item-by-Item Tests of Mean Differences (for Factor 3) by **Level of Education**

Education Level	30. Have clean and well maintained ships			25. Have ships which are comfortable to sail on			1. Have a modern fleet of ships			71. Have good cabin maintenance and cleaning facilities		
	Mean	Std. Dev	Sig. (p)	Mean	Std. Dev	Sig. (p)	Mean	Std. Dev	Sig. (p)	Mean	Std. Dev	Sig. (p)
Secondary School	6.27	0.82		5.96	1.08		5.99	1.02		6.17	0.84	
			* 0.01			* 0.03			0.14			0.11
University & Above	6.65	0.56		6.45	0.76		6.26	0.86		6.37	0.65	

*   Significant at 5% level

Item-by-Item Tests of Mean Differences (for Factor 3) by **Level of Education**

Education Level	2. Have attractive ambience and décor on their ships			74. Have ships which behave well at sea			23. Have spacious rooms to sleep and relax comfortably			68. Have good photo gallery facilities			35. Have fast check-in and check-out facilities		
	Mean	Std. Dev	Sig. (p)	Mean	Std. Dev	Sig. (p)	Mean	Std. Dev	Sig. (p)	Mean	Std. Dev	Sig. (p)	Mean	Std. Dev	Sig. (p)
Secondary School	6.23	0.89		5.86	1.19		5.10	1.08		5.20	1.42		5.12	1.57	
			0.10			* 0.00			* 0.00			* 0.03			0.07
University & Above	6.43	0.81		6.57	0.65		5.79	1.03		5.64	1.08		5.44	1.10	

* Significant at 5% level

Item-by-Item Tests of Mean Differences (for Factor 3) by **Type of Occupation**

Occupation Type	30. Have clean and well maintained ships			25. Have ships which are comfortable to sail on			1. Have a modern fleet of ships			71. Have good cabin maintenance and cleaning facilities		
	Mean	Std. Dev	Sig. (p)	Mean	Std. Dev	Sig. (p)	Mean	Std. Dev	Sig. (p)	Mean	Std. Dev	Sig. (p)
Not Working	6.15	0.86		5.74	1.24		5.88	1.02		6.02	0.87	
			* 0.00			* 0.00			* 0.03			0.07
Managerial	6.75	0.45		6.54	0.74		6.32	0.86		6.38	0.67	

* Significant at 5% level

Item-by-Item Tests of Mean Differences (for Factor 3) by **Type of Occupation**

Occupation Type	2. Have attractive ambience and décor on their ships			74. Have ships which behave well at sea			23. Have spacious rooms to sleep and relax comfortably			68.Have good photo gallery facilities			35. Have fast check-in and check-out facilities		
	Mean	Std. Dev	Sig. (p)	Mean	Std. Dev	Sig. (p)	Mean	Std. Dev	Sig. (p)	Mean	Std. Dev	Sig. (p)	Mean	Std. Dev	Sig. (p)
Not Working	6.21	0.84		5.57	1.49	*	5.19	1.21	*	5.38	1.22		5.05	1.34	*
Managerial	6.47	0.69	0.08	6.49	0.76	0.02	5.85	0.92	0.00	5.58	1.03	0.24	5.56	0.92	0.02

*   Significant at 5% level

132

				Mean Dif	Std Err	Sig
Factor 1	Scheffe	Twin	Triple	0.17	0.14	0.44*
			Quad	0.34	0.12	0.02*
		Triple	Twin	-0.17	0.14	0.44*
			Quad	0.17	0.15	0.53*
		Quad	Twin	-0.34	0.12	0.02*
			Triple	-0.17	0.15	0.53*
Factor 2	Scheffe	Twin	Triple	0.21	0.16	0.43*
			Quad	0.10	0.14	0.76*
		Triple	Twin	-0.21	0.16	0.43*
			Quad	-0.11	0.17	0.83*
		Quad	Twin	-0.10	0.14	0.76*
			Triple	0.11	0.17	0.83*
Factor 3	Scheffe	Twin	Triple	0.23	0.11	0.13*
			Quad	0.39	0.10	0.00*
		Triple	Twin	-0.23	0.11	0.13*
			Quad	0.16	0.12	0.45*
		Quad	Twin	-0.39	0.10	0.00*
			Triple	-0.16	0.12	0.45*
Factor 4	Scheffe	Twin	Triple	0.32	0.20	0.27*
			Quad	0.48	0.17	0.02*
		Triple	Twin	-0.32	0.20	0.27*
			Quad	0.16	0.21	0.74*
		Quad	Twin	-0.48	0.17	0.02*
			Triple	-0.16	0.21	0.74*

* The mean difference is significant at the .10 level.

Factor 1

		N	Subset for alpha = .10	
	In which category of cabin are you travelling on this cruise?		1.00	2.00
Student-Newman-Keuls	Quad	60.00	5.31	
	Triple	39.00	5.48	5.48
	Twin	90.00		5.65
	Sig.		0.22	0.19
Tukey B	Quad	60.00	5.31	
	Triple	39.00	5.48	5.48
	Twin	90.00		5.65
Scheffe	Quad	60.00	5.31	
	Triple	39.00	5.48	5.48
	Twin	90.00		5.65
	Sig.		0.47	0.43

Means for groups in homogeneous subsets are displayed.

a   Uses Harmonic Mean Sample Size = 56.160.

b   The group sizes are unequal. The harmonic mean of the group sizes is used. Type I error ▮ Are not guaranteed.

N	Subset for alpha = .10
	1.00
39.00	4.85
60.00	4.95
90.00	5.05
	0.38
39.00	4.85
60.00	4.95
90.00	5.05
39.00	4.85
60.00	4.95
90.00	5.05
	0.42

Factor 3

	In which category of cabin are you travelling on this cruise?	N	Subset for alpha = .10 1.00	2.00
Student-Newman-Keuls	Quad	60.00	5.83	
	Triple	39.00	5.99	
	Twin	89.00		6.22
	Sig.		0.17	1.00
Tukey B	Quad	60.00	5.83	
	Triple	39.00	5.99	
	Twin	89.00		6.22
Scheffe	Quad	60.00	5.83	
	Triple	39.00	5.99	5.99
	Twin	89.00		6.22
	Sig.		0.39	0.12

Means for groups in homogeneous subsets are displayed.

a   Uses Harmonic Mean Sample Size = 56.029.

b   The group sizes are unequal. The harmonic mean of the group sizes is used. Type I error Are not guaranteed.

Factor 4

	In which category of cabin are you travelling on this cruise?	N	Subset for alpha = .10 1.00	2.00

Student-Newman-Keuls	Quad	60.00	5.20	
	Triple	39.00	5.37	
	Twin	89.00		5.69
	Sig.		0.39	1.00
Tukey B	Quad	60.00	5.20	
	Triple	39.00	5.37	5.37
	Twin	89.00		5.69
Scheffe	Quad	60.00	5.20	
	Triple	39.00	5.37	5.37
	Twin	89.00		5.69
	Sig.		0.70	0.26

Means for groups in homogeneous subsets are displayed.

a   Uses Harmonic Mean Sample Size = 56.029.

b   The group sizes are unequal. The harmonic mean of the group sizes is used. Type I e

               Are not guaranteed.

Appendix 4 – Study three detailed analysis

RESPONDENTS BY GENDER

Gender	Frequency	Percent
Male	108	56.8%
Female	82	43.2%
Total	190	100%

RESPONDENTS BY MARITAL STATUS

Marital Status	Frequency	Percent
Single	66	34.7%
Married	110	57.9%
Divorced	11	5.8%
Widowed	3	1.6%
Total	190	100%

RESPONDENTS BY AGE

Age Group	Frequency	Percent
Below 25 yrs	34	17.9%
25 to 34 yrs	55	28.9%
35 to 44 yrs	57	30.0%
45 to 55 yrs	27	14.2%
55 and above	17	9.0%
Total	190	100%

RESPONDENTS BY INCOME

Income	Frequency	Percent
No income	47	24.7%
Less than $2000	22	11.6%
$ 2000 to $ 3500	42	22.1%
$ 3501 to $5000	27	14.2%
$ 5001 to $ 6500	27	14.2%
Above $ 6500	25	13.2%
Total	190	100%

RESPONDENTS BY EDUCATIONAL LEVEL

Education Level	Frequency	Percent
Secondary school	45	23.7%
A – Levels	30	15.8%
Polytechnic	43	22.6%
University	52	27.4%
Postgraduate	20	10.5%
Total	190	100%

RESPONDENTS BY OCCUPATION

Occupation	Frequency	Percent
Not working	44	23.2%
Clerical/Sales	19	10.0%
Supervisory	23	12.1%
Junior Executive	23	12.1%
Managerial	47	24.7%
Own Business	34	17.9%
Total	190	100%

RESPONDENTS BY PREVIOUS CRUISE EXPERIENCE

Type of Traveller	Frequency	Percent
Experienced	76	40.0 %
Inexperienced	114	60.0 %
Total	190	100 %

RESPONDENTS BY CLASS OF TRAVEL

Class of Travel	Frequency	Percent
Stateroom	127	67.2 %
Stateroom with balcony	57	30.2 %
Suite	5	2.6 %
Total	189	100 %

RESPONDENTS BY CABIN CATEGORY

Class of Travel	Frequency	Percent
Twin	90	47.6 %
Triple	39	20.6 %
Quad	60	31.8 %
Total	189	100 %

RESPONDENTS BY TRAVEL ACCOMPANIMENT

Travel Accompaniment	Frequency	Percent
Alone	2	1 %
With Family	109	57.4 %
In a Group	79	41.6 %
Total	190	100 %

Detailed Analysis of Multiple Regression – SERVQUAL and Customised Scales

Multiple Regression – SERVQUAL Dimensions and Word of Mouth

SERVQUAL Dimensions	B	Beta	t	Sig T
Tangibles	0.42	0.29	15.05	<.001*
Reliability	-0.05	-0.04	-2.06	0.04
Responsiveness	0.36	0.31	14.26	<.001*
Assurance	0.09	0.08	4.22	<.001*
Empathy	0.06	0.05	2.49	0.01*

F = 445.4   Sig. F = .000

* significant at 1% level

Multiple Regression – SERVQUAL Dimensions and Recommendation to others

SERVQUAL Dimensions	B	Beta	t	Sig T
Tangibles	0.37	0.26	14.00	<.001*
Reliability	0.03	0.02	1.10	0.27
Responsiveness	0.29	0.25	11.97	<.001*
Assurance	0.05	0.04	2.06	0.04
Empathy	0.17	0.15	7.35	<.001*

F = 510.0   Sig. F = .000

* significant at 1% level

Multiple Regression – SERVQUAL Dimensions and Future Patronage

SERVQUAL Dimensions	B	Beta	t	Sig T
Tangibles	0.32	0.17	8.57	<.001*
Reliability	0.16	0.11	4.64	<.001*
Responsiveness	0.52	0.35	15.66	<.001*
Assurance	-0.16	-0.12	-5.50	<.001*
Empathy	0.14	0.09	4.14	<.001*

F = 336.47   Sig. F = .000

* significant at 1% level

Multiple Regression – Factors of Customised Scale and Word of Mouth

Factors of Custom. Scale	B	Beta	t	Sig T
Liner Service Personnel	0.63	0.51	27.35	<.001*
On-board Services	0.07	0.06	3.79	<.001*
Operational Features	0.21	0.14	8.11	<.001*
Supplementary Services	-0.12	-0.15	-10.41	<.001*

F = 529.09   Sig. F = .000

* significant at 1% level

Multiple Regression – Factors of the Customised Scale and Recommendation to others

Factors of Custom. Scale	B	Beta	t	Sig T
Liner Service Personnel	0.41	0.33	18.48	<.001*
On-board Services	0.38	0.34	21.41	<.001*
Operational Features	0.14	0.09	5.76	<.001*
Supplementary Services	-0.06	-0.08	-5.91	<.001*

F = 629.42   Sig. F = .000

* significant at 1% level

Multiple Regression – Factors of the Customised Scale and Future Patronage

Factors of Custom. Scale	B	Beta	t	Sig T
Liner Service Personnel	0.49	0.32	16.94	<.001*
On-board Services	0.54	0.38	22.58	<.001*
Operational Features	-0.14	-0.07	-4.28	<.001*
Supplementary Services	0.00	0.01	0.21	0.83

F = 505.65   Sig. F = .000

* significant at 1% level

Test of Mean Differences in ratings of Behavioural Intentions by Demographic and Travel Behaviour variables

Tests of Mean Differences in ratings of Behavioural Intentions by Gender

Gender	Word-of-mouth			Recommendation to others			Future Patronage		
	Mean	Std. Dev	Sig. (p)	Mean	Std. Dev	Sig. (p)	Mean	Std. Dev	Sig. (p)
Male	5.97	0.92		5.83	0.87		5.26	1.09	
Female	5.90	0.91	0.04	5.87	0.93	0.19	5.62	1.19	<.001*

* significant at 1% level

Tests of Mean Differences in ratings of Behavioural Intentions by Marital Status

Marital Status	Word-of-mouth			Recommendation to others			Future Patronage		
	Mean	Std. Dev	Sig. (p)	Mean	Std. Dev	Sig. (p)	Mean	Std. Dev	Sig. (p)
Single	5.80	0.93		5.79	0.77		5.54	0.93	
Married	6.00	0.93	<.001*	5.90	0.97	<.001*	5.46	1.25	0.00*

* significant at 1% level

Tests of Mean Differences in ratings of Behavioural Intentions by Age

Age	Word-of-mouth			Recommendation to others			Future Patronage		
	Mean	Std. Dev	Sig. (p)	Mean	Std. Dev	Sig. (p)	Mean	Std. Dev	Sig. (p)
Below 25 years	5.66	1.02		5.82	0.77		5.60	0.83	
25 to 45 years	5.97	0.86	0.00*	5.82	0.89	<.001*	5.45	1.21	<.001*
Above 45 years	6.09	0.92		5.92	0.98		5.23	1.21	

* significant at 1% level

Tests of Mean Differences in ratings of Behavioural Intentions by Income

Income	Word-of-mouth			Recommendation to others			Future Patronage		
	Mean	Std. Dev	Sig. (p)	Mean	Std. Dev	Sig. (p)	Mean	Std. Dev	Sig. (p)
No Income	5.78	0.96		5.74	1.02		5.31	1.09	
Less than $5000	5.91	0.87	0.00*	5.89	0.77	<.001*	5.62	1.11	0.00*
More than $5000	6.17	0.91		5.85	0.96		5.17	1.22	

* significant at 1% level

Tests of Mean Differences in ratings of Behavioural Intentions by Education

Education	Word-of-mouth			Recommendation to others			Future Patronage		
	Mean	Std. Dev	Sig. (p)	Mean	Std. Dev	Sig. (p)	Mean	Std. Dev	Sig. (p)
Secondary School	5.86	0.99		5.88	1.05		5.66	1.11	
Polytechnic Dip.	5.88	0.84	<.001*	5.76	0.78	<.001*	5.39	1.09	0.00*
University & above	6.06	0.91		5.91	0.86		5.28	1.21	

* significant at 1% level

Tests of Mean Differences in ratings of Behavioural Intentions by Occupation

Occupation	Word-of-mouth			Recommendation to others			Future Patronage		
	Mean	Std. Dev	Sig. (p)	Mean	Std. Dev	Sig. (p)	Mean	Std. Dev	Sig. (p)
Not working	5.71	0.94		5.66	1.00		5.28	1.11	
Clerk/production/ Sales	5.95	0.96	0.00*	5.88	0.78	0.00*	5.64	0.91	0.00*
Managerial	5.97	0.87		5.82	0.79		5.35	1.14	
Own Business	6.17	0.89		6.12	0.97		5.64	1.29	

* significant at 1% level

Tests of Mean Differences in ratings of Behavioural Intentions by Previous Cruise Experience

Previous Cruise Experience	Word-of-mouth			Recommendation to others			Future Patronage		
	Mean	Std. Dev	Sig. (p)	Mean	Std. Dev	Sig. (p)	Mean	Std. Dev	Sig. (p)
Experienced	5.97	0.94	0.74	5.85	0.94	0.83	5.24	1.26	0.04*
Inexperienced	6.02	0.88		5.88	0.85		5.59	1.06	

* significant at 5% level

Tests of Mean Differences in ratings of Behavioural Intentions by Class of Travel

Class of Travel	Word-of-mouth			Recommendation to others			Future Patronage		
	Mean	Std. Dev	Sig. (p)	Mean	Std. Dev	Sig. (p)	Mean	Std. Dev	Sig. (p)
Stateroom	5.76	1.01		5.76	0.94		5.51	1.21	
Stateroom with balcony	5.98	0.94	0.12	5.84	0.87	0.72	5.19	1.17	0.10
Suite	6.25	0.50		6.00	0.71		4.50	0.58	

Tests of Mean Differences in ratings of Behavioural Intentions by Cabin Category

Cabin Category	Word-of-mouth			Recommendation to others			Future Patronage		
	Mean	Std. Dev	Sig. (p)	Mean	Std. Dev	Sig. (p)	Mean	Std. Dev	Sig. (p)
Twin	6.14	0.88		6.04	0.86		5.57	1.15	
Triple	5.84	0.78	0.13	5.65	0.76	0.03*	5.38	1.09	0.34
Quad	5.88	0.99		5.74	0.94		5.30	1.22	

* significant at 5% level

Tests of Mean Differences in ratings of Behavioural Intentions by Journey Accompaniment

Journey Accompaniment	Word-of-mouth			Recommendation to others			Future Patronage		
	Mean	Std. Dev	Sig. (p)	Mean	Std. Dev	Sig. (p)	Mean	Std. Dev	Sig. (p)
With Family	6.04	0.91		5.86	0.93		5.34	1.23	
In a Group	5.89	0.88	0.15	5.82	0.79	0.17	5.54	1.03	0.08

LIST OF REFERENCES

Aaker, D. A. (1992). The Value of Brand Equity. *Journal of Business Strategy, 13*(July/August), 27-32.

Ajzen, K., & Fishbein, M. (Eds.). (1980). *Understanding attitudes and predicting social behaviour*. Englewood Cliffs, N.J: Prentice-Hall.

Anderson, E. W., & Fornell, C. (1994). A Customer Satisfaction Research Prospectus. In R. T. Rust & R. L. Oliver (Eds.), *Service Quality: New Directions in Theory and Practice* (pp. 241-268). Thousand Oaks, CA: Sage Publications.

Anderson, E. W., & Sullivan, M. (1993). The Antecedents and Consequences of Customer Satisfaction for Firms. *Marketing Science, 12*(Spring), 125-143.

Atkinson, A. (1988). Answering the Eternal Question: What does the customer want? *Cornell HRA Quarterly, 30*(August).

Babakus, E., & Boller, G. W. (1992). An empirical assessment of the SERVQUAL scale. *Journal of Business Research, 24*, 253-268.

Barsky, J. D., & Labagh, R. (1992). A strategy for customer satisfaction. *Cornell HRA Quarterly, 33*, 32-37.

Berry, L. L., Zeithaml, V. A., & Parasuraman, A. (1996). The Behavioural Consequences of Service Quality. *Journal of Marketing, 60*(April), 31-46.

Bertrand, K. (1989). In Service Perceptions Count. *Business Marketing, 74*, 44-50.

Bitner, M. J., & Hubbert, A. R. (Eds.). (1994). *Service Quality: New Directions in Theory and Practice* Thousand Oaks, CA: Sage Publications.

Bolton, R. N., & Drew, J. H. (1991). A Multistage Model of Customers: Assessment of Service Quality and Value. *Journal of Consumer Research, 17*(March), 375-384.

Boulding, W., Kalra, A., Staelin, R., & Zeithaml, V. A. (1993). A Dynamic Process Model of Service Quality: From Expectations to Behavioural Intentions. *Journal of Marketing Research, 30*(Feb), 7-27.

Bovee, C., & Thill, J. (Eds.). (1992). *Marketing*: New York: McGraw-Hill.

Brown, J. R., & Fern, E. F. (Eds.). (1981). *Goods Vs Services Marketing: A Divergent Perspective* (Vol. 8): American Marketing, Chicago.

Brown, S. W., & Swartz, T. A. (1989). A Gap Analysis of Professional Service Quality. *Journal of Marketing, 53*(April), 92-98.

Buzzel, R. D., & Gale, B. T. (Eds.). (1987). *The PIMS Principles*: New York: The Free Press.

Buzzel, R. D., & Wiersema, F. D. (1991). Modeling Changes in Market Share: A Cross-Sectional Analysis. *Strategic Marketing Journal, 2*, 27-42.

Carlson, J. (1987). Moments of Truth. *Industry Week.*

Carman, J. M. (1990). Consumer Perceptions of Service Quality: An assessment of the SERVQUAL Dimensions. *Journal of Retailing, 66*(Spring), 33-55.

Chadee, D. D., & Mattson, J. (1996). An empirical assessment of customer satisfaction in tourism. *Services Industries Journal, 16*(3), 305-320.

Cronin, J. J., & Taylor, S. A. (1992). Measuring Service Quality: A Re-examination and Extension. *Journal of Marketing, 56*(July), 55-68.

Cronin, J. J., & Taylor, S. A. (1994). SERVPERF versus SERVQUAL: Reconciling Performance based and Perception based -minus - Expectation Measurements of Service Quality. *Journal of Marketing, 58*(January), 125-131.

Dahl, J. (1995, 11 August). Travel: Who go ashore when the ship's so nice. *Wall Street Journal.*

Dawkins, P., & Reichheld, F. (1990). Customer retention as a competitive weapon. *Directors and Boards, 14*(Summer), 42-47.

Day, G. S. (1990). *Market Driven Strategies: Processes for Creating Value*. New York: Macmillan Publications.

Deming, W. E. (Ed.). (1982). *Quality, Productivity and Compensation Position*: MIT Press, Cambridge, Masachusettes.

Desatnick, R. L. (Ed.). (1988). *Managing to keep customers*: Houghton Mifflin, Boston, M.A.

Enis, B. M., & Roering, K. J. (Eds.). (1981). *Services Marketing: Different Products, similar strategy*: American Marketing, Chicago.

Fick, G. R., & Ritchie, J. R. B. (1991). Measuring service quality in the travel and tourism industry. *Journal of Travel Research 30*(Fall), 2-9.

Fine, C. H. (1986). Quality Improvements and Learning in Productive Systems. *Management Science*(Oct), 686-705.

Finn, D. W., & Lamb, C. W. (1991). An evaluation of the SERVQUAL scales in retail setting. *Advances in Consumer Research, 18*.

Fornell, C., Johnson, M. D., Anderson, E. W., Cha, J., & Gryant, B. E. (1996). The American Customer Satifaction Index: Nature, Purpose and Findings. *Journal of Marketing, 60*, 7-18.

Fornell, C., & Wernerfelt, B. (1988). A Model for Customer Complaint Management. *Marketing Science, 7*(Summer), 271-286.

Gale, B. T. (1994). Managing Customer Value. *The Free Press*.

Gale, B. T., & Klavans, R. (1985). Formulating a quality improvement strategy. *Journal of Business Strategy*, 21-32.

Gamble, P., & Jones, P. (1991). Quality as a Strategic Issue. In *Strategic Hospitality Management*. London: Cassell.

Garvin, D. A. (Ed.). (1988). *Managing Quality*: Free Press, New York.

Genestre, A., & Herbig, P. (1997). Service Quality: an examination of demographic differences. *Journal of Customer Service in Marketing & Management, 3*(3), 65-83.

Goodfellow, J. H. (1983). The Marketing of Goods and Services as a Multi-dimensional Concept. *The Marketing Digest, Spring* 244-258.

Gorsuch, R. L. (Ed.). (1983). *Factor Analysis*: Hillsdale, N.J: Erlbaum.

Gourdin, K. N., & Kloppenborg, T. J. (1993). Identifying services gaps in commercial air travel: the first step towards quality improvement. *Transportation Journal, 31*(1), 22-30.

Gremler, D., Bitner, M. J., & Evans, K. R. (1994). The Internal Service Encounter. *International Journal of Service Industry Management, 5*, 34-56.

Gronroos, C. (Ed.). (1984). *Services Management and Marketing*: Massachusetts: Lexington Books.

Gronroos, C. (Ed.). (1991). *Services Management and Marketing*: Lexington Books: Massachusetts.

Hair, J. F., Anderson, R., Tatham, R., & Black, W. (Eds.). (1995). *Multivariate Data Analysis with Readings* (4th ed.): Prentice Hall International Inc.

Halstead, D., & Page, T. J. J. (1992). The effects of satisfaction and complaining behaviour on consumers repurchase behaviour. *Journal of Satisfaction, Dissatisfaction and Complaining Behaviour, 5*, 1-11.

Headly, D. E., & Miller, S. J. (1993). Measuring Service Quality and its Relationship to Future Consumer Behaviour. *Journal of Health Care Marketing, 13*(4), 32-41.

Hedderson, J., & Fisher, M. (Eds.). (1993). *SPSS Made Simple* (2nd ed.): Wasaworth Publishing Company.

Jarett, I. (1997). Cruise firms chart Asian waters. *Asian Business, Hongkong, Oct.*

Johnson, M. D., Anderson, E. W., & Fornell, C. (1995). Rational and adaptive performance expectations in a customer satisfaction framework. *Journal of Consumer Research, 21,* 695-707.

Kaiser, H. F. (1974, May 14). *Comments on communalities and the number of factors,* St Louis, Washington University.

Klein, M. (1996). Cruising for trouble. *American Demographics*(Nov).

Kotler, P. (1997). *Marketing Management: Analysis, Planning, Implementation and Control* (9th edition ed.). New Jersey: Prentice-Hall Inc.

Le Blanc, G. (1992). Factors affecting customer evaluation of service quality in Travel Agencies. *Journal of Travel Research, 30*(Spring), 10-16.

Lehtinen, U., & Lehtinen, J. R. (1982). Two approaches to service quality dimensions. *The Services Industries Journal, 2*(3), 287-303.

Lewis, B. R., & Mitchell, V. W. (1990). Defining and Measuring the Quality of Customer Service. *Marketing Intelligence and Planning, 8,* 11-17.

Lewis, R. C. (1994). The basics of hotel selection. *Cornell HRA Quarterly, 25*(May).

McCarthy, E. J., & Perrault, W. D. (Eds.). (1993). *Basic Marketing: A Global Managerial Approach*: Burr Ridge, IL: Richard D. Irwin.

McDougall, G. H., & Levesque, T. J. (1994). Benefit segmentation using service quality dimensions: an investigation in retail banking. *International Journal of Bank Management, 12*(2), 15-23.

McDougall, G. H. C., & Levesque, T. J. (2000). Benefit Segmentation using Service Quality Dimensions: An Investigation in Retail Banking. *International Journal of Bank Management, 12*(2), 15-23.

McKenna, J. T. (1990). Air Canada set to rebuild and compete in global market. *Aviation Week and Space Technology, May,* 37-38.

Mehta, S. C., & Vera, A. (1990). Segmentation in Singapore. *Cornell HRA Quarterly, 31*(May).

Morgan, N. A., & Piercy, N. F. (1992). Market-Led Quality. *Industrial Marketing Management, 21,* 111-118.

Murphy, I. P. (1996, January). Cruise lines float hopes on first time Customers. *Marketing News.*

Norusis, M. J. (Ed.). (1993). *SPSS for Windows: Advanced Statistics, Release 6.0.*

Nunnally, J. C., & Bernstein, I. H. (1994). *Psychometric Theory.* New York: McGraw-Hill Publishers.

Oliver, R. L. (1980). A Cognitive Model of the Antecedents and Consequences of Satisfaction Decisions. *Journal of Marketing Research, 17*(November), 460-469.

Oliver, R. L. (1981). Measurement and Evaluation of Satisfaction Process in Retail Settings. *Journal of Retailing, 57*(3), 25-48.

Oliver, R. L. (1997). *Satisfaction: A Behavioural Perspective on the Consumer.* New York: McGraw-Hill.

Ostrom, A., & Iacobucci, D. (1995). Consumer Trade-offs and the Evaluation of Services. *Journal of Marketing, 59*(January), 17-28.

Parasuraman, A., Zeithaml, V. A., & Berry, L. L. (1985). A Conceptual Model of Service Quality and its Implications for Future Research. *Journal of Marketing, 49*(Fall), 41-50.

Parasuraman, A., Zeithaml, V. A., & Berry, L. L. (1988). SERVQUAL: A Multiple-item Scale for Measuring Consumer Perceptions of Service Quality. *Journal of Retailing, 64*(1), 12-40.

Parasuraman, A., Zeithaml, V. A., & Berry, L. L. (1994). Reassessment of Expectations as a Comparison Standard in Measuring Service Quality: Implications for Future Research.

Journal of Marketing, 58(January), 111-124.

Philips, L. W., Chang, D. R., & Buzzell, R. D. (1983). Product Quality, Cost, Position and Business Performance. *Journal of Marketing, 47*, 26-43.

Pine, J., Victor, B., & Boynton, A. (1993). Making Mass Customisation work *Harward Business Review* Sept-Oct, 108-119.

Porter, M. E. (1985). *Competitive Advantage: Creating and Sustaining Performance*. New York: Free Press.

Prus, A., & Brandt, D. R. (1995). Understanding your Customers. *American Demographics*(Marketing Tools Supplement), 10-14.

Rathmell, J. M. (Ed.). (1974). *Marketing in the Services Sector*: Cambridge, Mass: Winthrop Publications.

Reichheld, F., & Sasser, J. W. E. (1990). Zero Defections:Quality comes to Services. *Harvard Business Review, 68*(September/October), 105-111.

Reid, R. D., & Sandler, M. (1992). The use of technology to improve service quality. *Cornell HRA Quarterly, 33*, 68-73.

Reidenbach, R. E., & Minton, A. P. (1991). Customer service segments: Strategic implications for the commercial banking industry. *Journal of Professional Marketing, 6*(2), 129-143.

Reidenbach, R. E., & Smallwood, B. S. (1990). Explaining perceptions of hospital operations by a modified SERVQUAL approach. *Journal of Health Care Marketing, 10*(December), 47-55.

Robertson, T. S., & Gatignon, H. (1986). Competitive effects on technology diffusion. *Journal of Marketing, 50*(July), 233-255.

Rushton, A. M., & Carson, D. J. (1985). The Marketing of Services: Managing the Tangibles. *European Journal of Marketing, 19*(3), 68-73.

Schiffman, L. G., & Kanuk, L. L. (Eds.). (1997). *Consumer Behaviour*: Upper Saddle River, N.J : Prentice Hall.

Shaw, S. (Ed.). (1994). *Airline Management* (3rd ed.): Pitman Publishing.

Shostack, L. C. (1978). The Services Marketing Frontier. *Review of Marketing, 11*, 373-388.

Stafford, M. R. (1996). Demographic discriminators of service quality in the banking industry. *Services Marketing, 10*(4), 6-22.

The Straits Times. (14 April 2000).

Swan, J. E., & Trawick, I. F. (1981). Disconfirmation of Expectations and Satisfaction with a retail service. *Journal of Retailing, 57*, 48-67.

Teas, R. K. (1993). Consumer perceptions and the measurement of Service Quality. *Journal of Professional Services Marketing, 8*, 33-54.

Times, T. S. (2000, 14th April).

Vandamme, R., & Leunis, J. (1992). *Development of a multi-item scale for the measuring of hospital service quality*. Paper presented at the Second International Research Seminar in Service Management.

Watson, C. J., Billingsley, P., Croft, D. J., & Huntsberger, D. V. (Eds.). (1993). *Statistics for Management & Economics*: Allyn & Bacon.

Webster, C. (1989). Can consumers be segmented on the basis of their service quality expectations. *Journal of Services Marketing, 3*(2), 35-53.

Westbrook, R. A., & Oliver, R. L. (1991). The dimensionality of consumption emotion patterns and consumer satisfaction. *Journal of Consumer Research, 18*, 84-91.

Woodruff, R. B., Cadotte, E. R., & Jenkins, R. L. (1983). Modeling consumer satisfaction processes using experience-based norms. *Journal of Marketing Research, 20*, 296-304.

Woodside, A., Frey, L., & Daly, R. (1989). Linking Service Quality, Customer Satisfaction and Behavioral Intentions. *Journal of Health Care Marketing, 9*(December), 5-17.

Wulfsberg, R., & Pulaski, D. (1990). It takes more than a simple survey to measure customer satisfaction. *Marketing News, 24*(11), 14.

Yu, L. (1992). Seeing stars: China's hotel-rating system. *Cornell HRA Quarterly, 33*, 24-27.

Zahorik, A. J., & Rust, R. T. (1993). Customer satisfaction, customer retention and market share. *Journal of Retailing, 69*(2 (Summer)), 103-125.

Zeithaml, V. A., Berry, L. L., & Parasuraman, A. (1993). The Nature and Determinants of Customer Expectations of Service. *Journal of the Academy of Marketing Science, 21*(1), 1-12.

Zeithaml, V. A., Berry, L. L., & Parasuraman, A. (1996). The Behavioral Consequences of Service Quality. *Journal of Marketing, 60*(April), 31-42.

Zeithaml, V. A., & Bitner, M. J. (Eds.). (2000). *Services Marketing: Integrating customer focus across the firm* (2nd ed.): Irwin McGraw-Hill, London.

Scientific Publishing House

offers

free of charge publication

of current academic research papers, Bachelor´s Theses, Master's Theses, Dissertations or Scientific Monographs

If you have written a thesis which satisfies high content as well as formal demands, and you are interested in a remunerated publication of your work, please send an e-mail with some initial information about yourself and your work to *info@vdm-publishing-house.com.*

Our editorial office will get in touch with you shortly.

VDM Publishing House Ltd.
Meldrum Court 17.
Beau Bassin
Mauritius
www.vdm-publishing-house.com

Printed by
Schaltungsdienst Lange o.H.G., Berlin